Ghost Whisperer Suzie

Heaven on Earth

Suzie Price

BALBOA.
PRESS

A DIVISION OF HAY HOUSE

Balboa Press books may be ordered through booksellers or by contacting:

Balboa Press
A Division of Hay House
1663 Liberty Drive
Bloomington, IN 47403
www.balboapress.com.au
1 (877) 407-4847

Because of the dynamic nature of the Internet, any web addresses or links contained in this book may have changed since publication and may no longer be valid. The views expressed in this work are solely those of the author and do not necessarily reflect the views of the publisher, and the publisher hereby disclaims any responsibility for them.

The author of this book does not dispense medical advice or prescribe the use of any technique as a form of treatment for physical, emotional, or medical problems without the advice of a physician, either directly or indirectly. The intent of the author is only to offer information of a general nature to help you in your quest for emotional and spiritual well-being. In the event you use any of the information in this book for yourself, which is your constitutional right, the author and the publisher assume no responsibility for your actions.

Any people depicted in stock imagery provided by Thinkstock are models, and such images are being used for illustrative purposes only.
Certain stock imagery © Thinkstock.

Printed in the United States of America.

ISBN: 978-1-4525-1280-8 (sc)
ISBN: 978-1-4525-1279-2 (e)

Balboa Press rev. date: 04/02/2014

To my loving mother, Sandra, who brought
me into this life and raised me.

I know you are not perfect but you have done your best
and I appreciate everything you have done for me.

Love you, Mum xx

Contents

Acknowledgements

My heartfelt thanks go to Greg Beutel, who helped with the editing and content of this book, and to my loving husband, Stephen Price, who contributed so much to the writing of this book and without whom this book may not have been finished.

Introduction

My name is Suzie Price, and I am one of Australia's top psychic mediums and spiritual teachers. As a professional medium, I have been doing private readings for over fifteen years, doing psychic shows for over six years, and running courses for the last four years. I have appeared on *Psychic TV* during its first year in Australia and have been filmed in many investigations as the main medium for Haunted Australia. I have also had quite a bit of exposure on radio, in magazines, and in newspapers. Much of my life has been dedicated to helping others with my abilities and developing my spiritual knowledge and sharing it with others.

As a psychic medium, I talk to spirits. I see angels and ghosts walk beside us, and I connect people with spirits who are departed loved ones. These spirits give me insights into the future and past as I tap into the energies between the world of the living and the spirit world. I discovered my abilities after a near-death experience as a child, but I didn't use my gifts until much later in my late twenties, starting professionally in my early thirties. With development and tuning, my gifts have shaped me into the person I am today. I am a soft, gentle, and loving person who is very sensitive in many ways, and I hold strong spiritual beliefs. Many people have suggested many times that I write a book, so here it is.

I have written this book to explain what I do as a psychic medium and to share with you the good, the bad, and the ugly stories from my life. Along the way, I've tried to explain my beliefs, my abilities, and my understanding of spirituality, and I've also tried to give you some insight into how you can develop your own abilities and grow spiritually.

I hope to inspire you to reach for your dreams and be the best you can be. I hope you can find the secret to success and happiness in your own life, like I have. I also wish to encourage you to strive to overcome the biggest obstacles life can throw at you and come out smiling. My life has not been easy, and it has taken me a long time to get to where I am now with help from many people. I have learnt many lessons on my journey so far, and whatever may come in the future, I welcome it with love.

I do not intend to force my opinions or beliefs on others; however, as I share them, I hope that you'll connect with the book and take something from it that inspires you in your journey through this life.

This book contains my private experiences, including those with many people who are or have been close to me or who have impacted my life. I've tried to be honest about what has happened in my life. These experiences have shaped me into the person I am today, and I hold no negative feelings towards any of them or the people I've experienced them with. I've put the past behind me, and I'm grateful for everything I have gone through. I ask all of those who read this book not to judge those I've written about, as my view of these experiences don't define these people.

It was not as easy to recall many events from early in my life as it was to recall those from more recent times. However, I have done the best that my memory would allow and have managed to piece together a reasonably accurate account of my life up to where I am today.

As I really had no idea what to say or what to write about, my husband, Stephen Price, has helped me with much of this book, suggesting topics to write about and also helping me with the wording. It is really only because of his support and encouragement that I both started and finished this book. He contributed so much to this book in many ways, and I wish to thank him for all his hard work over many hours.

I want to thank so many people who have helped and inspired me on my life's journey: in addition to Stephen, I thank my mum; my stepdad, Gary; my nan; my children; and all of my good friends for all the love and support they have given and continue to give to me. I also give thanks to all of my clients and to all the lessons that have made me who I am. Of course, I offer a special thank you to all my guides, spirits, and angels and to God/Goddess, the creator.

Chapter 1

My Origins

To give you proper understanding of who I am, where I came from, and how I got to where I am now, it's best to start at the beginning.

I was born Suzie Daubert in King George Hospital, Sydney, New South Wales, on 30 July 1968, the only child to Sandra Hallesy and Michael George Daubert. I weighed seven pound and six ounces. My mother described me as a beautiful baby; I had big blue eyes and blonde hair, and I was a normal healthy girl.

My mother was twenty-one when I was born and had only been married to my father for about a year. The marriage did not last long after that, as she left him when I was just six weeks old. My mother felt she wasn't supported by my father emotionally or financially. At the time, he couldn't hold down a full-time job, and she didn't want to live week to week not knowing whether he would earn the money to support us. I'm not sure about the exact details of what happened between them, and I have never heard my father's side of the story, but my mother is a very determined and strong woman, and I know she did what she felt was right for herself and for me. I also know that my mother loved my father, as she has said that he was the love of her life. Whatever her reason for leaving my father was, it was her choice to leave, and I'm sure what happened unfolded as it was meant to.

After the first few weeks of my life, I met my father only one time that I remember. I am told he came to see me when I was three years old, but I have no memory of that visit. I do remember that when I was nine years old, he arranged to spend a day with me. He took me to Luna Park, a big amusement park in Sydney. I was nervous and uncomfortable, as I didn't know him. I didn't want to see him, but my mother told me I had to, as he was my father and he really wanted to see his daughter. Reluctantly, I went with him, but I was shy and reserved, and my attitude towards him was generally negative, and I am sure he felt this. He was kind, gentle, and very loving towards me, and I realized that I looked very much like him. We had a good day, and I did enjoy myself, but I was glad to get back home to Mum.

I wish that I had been nicer to him on that day, and when I got older, I wanted to meet him again to get to know him better, but unfortunately, I have had no contact with him since then. I tried to find him for many years once I was old enough. I located his sister, Margaret Daubert, in Alberta, Canada. I phoned her on a few occasions, and we corresponded in letters and emails for a time. I asked her if she knew where my father was, but she said he didn't want me to contact him and didn't give me any details about his whereabouts.

My mother struggled as a single mother for the first couple of years of my life. We lived in a flat in Sydney until I was almost two years old, when we moved into her parents' house in Drummoyne. Also living there at this time were my mother's younger brothers, Terry (nine at that time) and Gary (who was six weeks younger than me) and my mother's younger sister Dorna, although she moved out a few years later, when I was still quite young, so I don't remember much about the time when she was there.

My grandparents, William Daniel and Patricia Joyce Hallesy, were like a second mum and dad to me, and I had a very strong bond with them both. My grandfather was born in Wales and my grandmother was born in Wallasey, Cheshire, England. They had moved to Australia in their mid-twenties with my mother and two uncles after they lost their third child in an accident. In Australia, they had three more children. William, my pop, found work that included carrying big bags of asbestos fibre.

Mum never wanted to have more children after me. She felt that she had had enough of raising children, as from a young age, she had been required to help her mum clean the house and take care of all of her brothers and her sister because her father was old-fashioned and believed that only women should do housework.

Mum and I lived with my grandparents for the next ten years, until I was twelve years old. I went to Drummoyne Public School with my uncle Gary. He and I grew up like brother and sister; when we were little, people thought we were twins. Gary was a very gentle boy, but I was quite lively and had a bit of a naughty streak. When Gary and I would each get a bag of lollies, I would eat all of mine straight away, and Gary would play with his, taking them out of the bag and carefully rolling them on the carpet like little balls. I would quickly pick them up and eat them all. This made Gary very upset, and my grandmother never let me forget about this, as I did this on quite a few occasions.

A loving couple, Harry and Betty, lived a few houses up from Nan's and next door to Harry's twin sister. Harry and Betty had no children of their own, and they spoiled me. I often went to their place to play, and they would give me lots of treats to eat and buy me presents. They even put a swimming pool in their backyard for me. I have a lot of fond memories of spending time at their home throughout my childhood, and I loved them dearly. They were like another set of parents whose only job was to spoil me, and I loved the attention.

My mother was very loving, and although money was very tight for her as a single mum, she always managed to take good care of me. My mum and grandmother often took Gary and me on outings to parks and playgrounds. These were always happy times, as I loved playing at the parks and being pushed on the swings.

When Mum or Nan were angry with me, I would hide, often behind the lounge, because I was scared of being yelled at or spanked, not that much actual spanking took place. I really didn't like being yelled at or getting into trouble with Mum or Nan, and I always cried when I did. Even back then, I was quite sensitive and got upset easily.

As a young child, I was quite outgoing and adventurous. I was very bubbly and would talk to anyone and everyone. My mother told me that as a toddler, I would leave the house when she wasn't looking and go on little adventures, leaving her distraught with worry as she frantically searched for me. I did this enough that she pushed a cupboard in front of the doors so I couldn't open them and get out.

My mother often told me that I had no fear of anything when I was little, but all that, and my whole life, changed when I had my accident.

At the age of seven, I was walking home from school with Uncle Terry, who was sixteen, and Uncle Gary. We stopped at a traffic light, and when the walk light came on, we began crossing the road, with Terry and Gary in the lead. I wasn't holding the book I was carrying properly, and it slipped out of my hands and dropped to the ground. I stopped and bent to pick it up, but I didn't notice a car coming, and the driver didn't see me or the red light and didn't stop. Her car hit me.

The car sent my little body flying through the air, and I landed on the ground a few metres in front of the car. I was unconscious.

While I was unconscious, I had what I can only describe as a near-death experience. I will always remember this vividly, as it seemed so real. I envisioned a luminous being, which I believe was an angel, although I don't remember seeing wings. She was the most beautiful lady I have ever seen: she was tall and had striking blue eyes and long, flowing blonde hair. She embraced me, and as she held me, I felt deep love, like the love from my mother only one hundred times more intense. I felt safe, protected, and extremely happy. It was like the angel had always known me and had always been near, as she felt familiar. She comforted me and told me not to worry because everything was fine and I would be all right.

I wanted to stay with her and experience this ultimate bliss forever, but she told me that I had to go back. However, she said that she would always be with me and that from then on, I would be quite different to other children, as I would experience, see, and feel things many other people wouldn't understand. This confused me. *Why do I have to go?* I thought. *Why can't I stay? What does she mean?*

The next thing I knew, my eyes were open. It all seemed like some kind of dream, but at the same time it felt very real, and my confusion remained. Then, all of a sudden, I felt intense pain and could not talk, and I saw blood all over me. The car must have hit me in the face first. I had sustained a bad concussion, a fractured jaw, broken teeth, and many bad bruises, cuts, scratches, and other wounds. Terry had told Gary to run home to get my nan, and Terry then rushed over to me. I'm not sure how long I was unconscious, but I estimate almost ten minutes, as it would have taken Gary that long to go home, get Nan, and come back. Nan was there just after I came to.

Terry sat on the ground with me trying to hold me as he cried and yelled at the woman who had hit me. I'm told that she said she hadn't seen the red light or me because the sun was in her eyes, but looking back now, I realize that the sun would have been behind her at the time of the accident, so she must not have been paying proper attention. She was also crying, and I think she was in shock as well; she kept saying, "I'm so sorry!"

On-lookers were everywhere, and some tried to help. Uncle Terry seemed to be the most upset. I was in a daze as this all happened, and I kept looking for the angel I had seen, thinking, *Where did that lady go?*

A moment later, Gary returned with Nan and Pop, and the next thing I knew, I was being picked up by Pop and put into the back seat of the car that had hit me. They had decided not to wait for an ambulance, as the hospital wasn't far away. I lay on the back seat with my head on Nan's lap, and she held a towel or cloth to my head to staunch the bleeding.

Back at the scene, Pop took my uncles home and called my mum at work, and then they picked my mum up and came to the hospital.

The doctors cleaned up the blood and tended to my injuries, including wiring my jaw. I visited the dental hospital in Sydney many times after this to have my teeth fixed.

The doctor said I was quite a little miracle; he was amazed that I hadn't sustained major injuries or been killed, but I knew the angel had saved me. I stayed in the hospital overnight, and the next day, I was allowed to go home with bandages wrapped around my head and over the abrasions on my arms and legs. I still felt a lot of pain and had to have a few weeks off school. Because my jaw was wired, I had trouble talking and took my food through a straw, which was horrible, but I did get to eat lots of ice cream, which was good.

Following the accident, I was different from other children; it was like something inside me had changed. I was no longer a bright, bubbly, outgoing child who was adventurous and knew no fear; I became a lot more quiet, reserved, timid, and even more sensitive.

At night, I had vivid dreams of spiritual beings, particularly the angel who had been with me through the accident. She connected with me regularly throughout my childhood. She was very much like a mother protecting her child from harm, so loving and caring, and she was so beautiful, always smiling and radiating gold and white light. The dreams seemed real, but when I told Mum and Nan about them, they would say, "It is only a dream, and dreams aren't real." I started to draw, paint, and collect statues of angels. I was still unsure of what these experiences meant, but I knew deep down inside the spiritual beings I saw protected and divinely guided me.

Not long after the dreams began, I started seeing angels and spirits when I was awake as well. At first I sometimes saw faces when I looked into dark rooms, shadowy places, or windows at night. As I lay in bed at night, I also saw these faces, but they weren't frightening at all. They would smile and watch me, and I somehow knew they were nice and meant no harm.

Then, after a while, the faces became people, and I could see them at any time of day or night. At first they stood around not doing much, but before long, they sat and talked with me. These spirits and angels comforted me and reassured me that everything was okay. Most of the time I thought of these spiritual entities as real people who were there in the room with me and talking to me like any other person. I was never afraid of them, and I always felt love from them.

I didn't understand these experiences, and when I tried to explain to my mother what was going on, she took me to doctors, counsellors, and psychologists to figure out what was happening. She explained that I talked to people when no one was there, like I had imaginary friends. Each professional then asked me who I was talking to, and I told them that I talked to people all the time but no one else could see them. These professionals believed it was all in my head, and said to my mum I was an overly emotional child with a very vivid imagination affected by the accident, but they assured my mum this was nothing to worry about and that I would grow out of it.

By this time, I saw spirits everywhere, including at school, and school became quite difficult. I picked up the emotions and energies of others, receiving insights into other people's lives that could be quite disturbing, to the point that I even fainted. I could hear voices and would see images of people at different times in their lives, some I knew and some I had never seen before. Often I would look at someone and they had other people standing around them. They smiled at me, and I didn't realize they were actually spirits. When I tried to tell people anything about this, they thought I was crazy. No one believed me.

Before long, the kids talked about me, and many of them teased me, called me names, and laughed at me. This affected me deeply and made me scared to talk about it. The kids stayed away from me unless they were making fun of me. There were three particularly nasty girls who seemed to go out of their way to bully me, and they continued to do so for many years throughout primary school and into high school. I hated them, and I hated going to school because of the fear that they would pick on me. The bullying affected me deeply, and I would often cry because of it, and it made me scared to talk about my experiences.

Uncle Gary did his best to help me fit in and to involve me in activities with his friends, and this helped me a lot. Gary had become very outgoing, so I felt safe when with him, as I didn't have to talk to others about what I was experiencing. However, more and more, I refused to go to school and thus spent a lot of time at home. This was fine with me since no one could hurt me or tease me there, but Mum got angry and yelled at me for not wanting to go to school. This upset me and made me cry, and I would spend most of the day in my room afterwards. But I was never truly alone, as angels and spirits were always near me, and staying home gave me time to get to know them better.

I became quite lonely and isolated, as I kept away from the other kids. My fainting spells became quite frequent when I did go to school, and I spent a lot of time in the sick bay. Thinking back, I now see that these fainting episodes as a coping mechanism, a protective defence, but they also gave my schoolmates another reason to tease me.

The accident really affected Uncle Terry as well. He blamed himself for what had happened to me and suffered from severe depression, and he used drugs as an escape from his guilt. He eventually became addicted and moved out of Nan and Pop's place. About ten years after the accident, when he was twenty-seven and living in Melbourne, he committed suicide by hanging himself.

Out of all of the spirits who visited me, four in particular, stayed with me most of the time, and I came to learn that they were my guides. The first, Trisha, appeared to be an islander; she looked about forty-eight years of age with dark, tight curls and dark skin with a big beautiful smile. She was also loving and motherly and visited me in my dreams, and often when I was awake. I still feel her presence with me constantly, and I know she is there to help me, especially when I'm upset or going through something major. I see her as being my main spirit guide.

My second guide, Arlenea, is tall and slender with dark hair. She informed me that she lived in the 1700s as a medicine woman or shamanic healer, she healed the poor and the sick, so when I or my friends or family feel unwell, I call on Arlenea for help, and she is always there.

The third guide is Crystal: angelic with blonde hair, blue eyes, and a pure divine essence. She told me she never had an earthly life because she is one of God's divine helpers, sending love and guidance to souls who pass over. She came to help me with communication with spirits and often accompanied spirits who would talk to me.

The fourth guide is Aaron, who appears to be about twenty-eight years old tall and is muscular with fair hair. He is a warrior and protector like Archangel Michael. He protects me whenever I'm in danger, and he gives me inner strength when I need it.

Throughout my childhood, I often saw these guides watching over me, and sometimes I talked with them. I would often look out the window to find them sitting in the tree outside. I now have many more guides and see these four less often than I did when I was young.

Whilst I was still in primary school, my grandfather became quite ill with asbestosis as a result of the job he had carrying asbestos fibre. He had to stop working, which made things very hard for my family financially.

When I was eleven, my mother met a man named Gary Cox and fell in love, and after a year of dating, they got married. They had a small ceremony at the registry office and then a reception in the back yard at Nan and Pop's. After the wedding, Mum and I moved out of Nan and Pop's home and into a unit in Gladesville, outside of Sydney, with Gary. I was sad to leave Nan and Pop and Uncle Gary, as I was so close to them, but I was also excited for Mum and knew I would still see my relatives.

My stepfather, Gary, was a lovely man, and as he had no children of his own, he became quite fond of me. Gary became a loving stepfather, and I was so happy that Mum had found someone.

The following year, I went to Riverside Girls High in Gladesville. Things were a little better in high school, but I still hated school, as the same three girls still picked on me and teased me a lot. My fainting spells continued, and I still picked up on energy and emotions from the other kids, but I would try to ignore it and wouldn't talk about it with anyone. I still felt like a loner, but I made a couple of close friends, Pauline and Tracey, who made school much easier. Pauline, my closest friend, had a great sense of humour and made me laugh. She was also pretty and popular, and everyone at school liked her. When I was with her, the bullies didn't hassle me as much, which was great. Pauline and I spent a lot of time together at each other's homes, at the beach, at the movies, and at other places, and on occasion, her mum and dad took me on holidays. We had a lot of fun together.

Tracey was a bit of a troubled soul. Her dad was an alcoholic and abusive. I don't remember ever going inside her house; I only met her outside when we would go out together or see her at school. Tracey often seemed quite agitated but never talked much about what was going on at home.

Tracey and I were both good runners and both did well in long-distance races in high school. I loved to go ice-skating with her at the Macquarie Centre in Ryde, near Sydney, and I became quite good at speed-skating, doing twirls, and skating backwards. I discovered boys at this time and had my first crush on a boy I knew from the ice-skating rink called Craig. We dated a few times, and he was the first boy I ever kissed.

When I was fourteen, Pop received a compensation payout, as he had been one of the first people to sue for compensation because of his illness. The payout wasn't huge, but it was enough for him, and at the time, he was becoming too ill to continue pushing for a settlement through to the high court. With the money, Nan and Pop bought a house in Lawson, in the Blue Mountains, and moved from Drummyone.

Then, when I was fourteen years and nine months old, I left school in year nine as I just couldn't handle it any more. The bullying had continued, and so had my fainting spells, and I suffered anxiety and depression. I tried to ignore the energy I picked up on from others more and more.

When I told my teachers I was leaving school, the PE teacher told me I would never amount to anything! This upset me, but her lack of empathy didn't surprise me, as she and my other teachers had done little to help me with the bullying I endured. I was so happy the day I left school, and I never looked back.

Not long afterwards, Mum, Gary, and I moved to Kogarah, another suburb of Sydney, and I got my first job. I didn't have much to choose from with my lack of skills, but I answered an ad for a sales assistant at a newsagent in Leichardt and got the job. I worked full-time, five days a week, and I quickly learnt how to do all the tasks I had to do, and I really enjoyed working there. The boss was kind to me, and I liked earning my own money. I didn't see my friends very often, as they were still at school, but we met up some weekends.

I still had a lot of insecurities. I was quite shy, so I didn't talk to people much, and I often sat alone, worrying about what other people thought about me or, even more, about how they might treat me. I didn't like being yelled at or teased or put down. I felt I couldn't trust people.

Four months after I started work at the newsagent, Pop's health became much worse, and Nan struggled to look after him, so Mum, Gary, and I moved to Lawson to live with Nan, Pop, and Uncle Gary, who was in year ten at Katoomba High School. I got to know Uncle Gary's friends, who were quite nice, and his friend Paul became my first real boyfriend. We dated for about six months.

When we first moved, I travelled to my job in Leichardt. I got up at about 5:00 a.m. and caught a train from Lawson to Central Station, where I caught a bus to Leichardt. I loved the job and found it to be a great learning experience, but I left soon after we moved because the commute was too much for me.

Pop's illness then became so bad that he had to be placed in a nursing home in Wentworth Falls. Although the family and I visited him often, this was a very emotional time for me because I was so close to Pop. I still remember his big blue eyes, his good looks that Nan said were just like Errol Flynn's, and his broad Welsh accent. Pop had been happiest sitting in the backyard in the sunshine drinking his homemade brew and smoking his hand-rolled cigarettes. It was hard to see the health of such a strong man decline as his did. Not long after moving to the home, after battling his whole life, Pop passed away. Rest peacefully, my beautiful poppy. I love you. I wrote this song for you:

I'd Give My Breath To You
Copyright Apra 1998

Verse 1

I'd give my breath to you.
I feel so helpless; what can I do?
I'd give my life to you
So I can say I love you
You're lying there with eyes so closed,
But your body still feels warm
If you'd wake I'd smile at you,
And I'd give my breath to you.

Verse 2

I'd give my breath to you.
I feel so helpless; what can I do?
I think about the times gone by;
There's still so much to say to you.
I need to tell you how you saved my life,
And I'd give my breath to you.

Repeat verse 1 three times.

After Poppy passed, his spirit visited me in my sleep to reassure me that he was fine, and I often heard the song "Danny Boy." I knew that was a sign from Pop because his name was Daniel, and he was called Danny by his friends.

Mum, Gary, and I moved to Penrith not long after Poppy passed away, and when Uncle Gary finished high school, he and Nan also moved to Penrith, to a little unit Nan bought not far away from my house. Uncle Gary and I both got jobs at Gowings, a menswear shop in Sydney. Gary worked in the clothing section and I worked at the cigarette bar. This is where I met my next boyfriend, Steve, when I was sixteen. He worked in the shoe department upstairs, and we fell in love at first sight.

I had always loved to sing, and I sang along with the radio or unaccompanied while I was doing things at home. Mum had always told me that I had a lovely voice, and a few friends had also told me this, so I decided to develop my voice so I could perform onstage. I found a singing teacher, and I started singing lessons at the Johnny Young Talent School. My singing teachers name was Don and I really looked forward to my singing lessons every week.

These lessons helped me come out of my shell and regain some of my confidence. The lessons continued for the next four years, and my singing improved immensely through my lessons with Don, and I learnt how to better control my voice and perform.

I started performing at talent quests and karaoke competitions reaching the semi-finals many times and also winning at different clubs around Sydney. Although getting up onstage to sing was nerve-racking, I really loved to do it, and I loved the praise I received. Mum and Gary were always so proud of me after I performed. I was so happy that I set my eyes on becoming a famous singer.

I tried to cut myself off from the psychic messages I received and didn't talk about my ability with my boyfriend or friends. I just wanted to be a normal teenager and to have fun. However, at night, I still had vivid dreams of angels, and spirit people as well as Pop wanted to communicate with me. It was nice to know they still loved me, and even though I told them to go away, they never gave up on me. Gradually, I saw them less and less, and the way they appeared changed. Now, I saw them not as people standing next to me but as glimpses of spirits or images of them in my mind. I can sometimes still see them in the room with me or standing near other people, but the image last usually just for a few moments or is in my mind's eye.

When I was seventeen, Mum, Gary, and I moved back to Kogarah. I went to a technical and further education (TAFE) college there to finish my school certificate. I enjoyed the school and found learning there much more comfortable and easy than it has been at my previous school. I completed my year ten certificate, and a couple of months later, I also completed a typing course and then a computer course at a business college nearby. While I was going to TAFE, I became friends with Julie and Natasha, lovely girls who I sometimes went out with. I started to go to night clubs in Sydney with Julie and another friend named Danielle. Julie, Danielle, and I were like the Three Musketeers. We loved dancing at the clubs and had wonderful nights out together. I was really starting to enjoy my life. When I was eighteen, I moved into a flat with Julie for about six months, but then I moved back home because of a lack of money.

I had a few boyfriends on and off in these years, but no serious relationships. I saw Nan every few weeks and Uncle Gary from time to time, and I went out with my friends quite regularly. I really matured into a young lady. I felt proud of myself for going to technical college and completing my school certificate and the other courses, and I was also proud of myself for continuing to develop my singing.

Despite my growing confidence, I was still full of insecurity, and I didn't know what I wanted to do with my life. I tried out a few different jobs, but I never lasted long in any of them, as if I didn't like the work or the people I worked with, I left. I liked the idea of being a professional singer, but I didn't know if I was good enough, and if I was, I had no idea how to pursue this career. I didn't put my mind to anything except making plans with friends. We went to movies and night clubs, where men often bought us drinks, and the attention made me feel better about myself.

Over the years, Nan and Mum had come to accept that I had more than a vivid imagination, and they become more curious about spirits and psychic phenomena. I was also intrigued by psychic things, and found that I was drawn to the subject more and more as I grew older. Nan and I had our first tarot-card reading when I was seventeen, and I had a tea-leaf reading after that. Both of these made some sense to my life and I could relate to some of the information, but they didn't reveal what I was hoping for and expecting, as I felt the information should have been more specific than it was. I wanted to know more. Nan and I went to several other psychics in the following eighteen months, and I enjoyed all the readings I received and was intrigued that the psychics knew certain things. Some of what I was told related to my past and some of the events the psychics predicted did happen. One psychic that I saw around this time told me that I would become rich and famous when I was in my forties. I liked this idea, so I've held onto this thought since then. However, in each reading, much of the information I received made no sense or was just plain wrong.

At the age of eighteen, I saw a television show featuring adults and children who had had near-death experiences in which they felt the presence of and saw angels helping them, and these people shared their drawings, paintings, and statues of angels. Each person's story was different, but they were all similar to my experience. Finally, I had found others like me, and I felt a sense of belonging and had a greater understanding of myself. A weight had been lifted off my shoulders. I felt a renewed connection with the spirits and angels I saw, and I also felt a strong need to connect more with God, so I bought books to teach me more about God, angels, and spirits and read them in my spare time.

When I was twenty, I was dancing with a girlfriend at a nightclub when a well-dressed and reasonably handsome guy, who said his name was Craig, came over and started dancing with me. He seemed quite nice, and after a few dances, he bought me drinks and we talked. We had a good time, so we arranged to see each other again. We went on a few dates, and soon we were boyfriend and girlfriend, and after we had been seeing each other for about six months, he asked me to move in with him.

We shared a rental house with another couple who were nice enough. The woman, a friend of Craig's, was very pretty, with long, straight blonde hair; a slim figure; and big breasts. Craig had other friends who also looked like this, and he constantly looked at their bodies, and would comment to me on how hot they looked, and compare me to them, complaining that my hair wasn't as nice as theirs or that my breasts weren't as big as theirs. It seemed like he did this constantly, and it made me angry at him and jealous of these women.

While I was living with Craig, I got a job as a secretary in an investment firm in Bondi. This was a great job with a nice boss, and I really enjoyed it and was good at it. Craig worked for himself sewing canvas canopies for boats, and he was quite good at it and was always busy. I felt happy some of the time I spent with Craig, but his constant put-downs about my appearance really affected my self-image and made me depressed at times.

I was a size 10 at the time, and he criticized my body in particular, suggesting that I was putting weight on when I wasn't or complaining that my breasts were too small and suggesting I get a boob job. His negativity affected our relationship and caused fights, and sometimes when he became angry he quite aggressively yelled at me and verbally abused me. I became afraid that I would do something that made him angry, as I worried he would hit me, and on a number of occasions, he did slap me and hurt me, although not hard enough to leave a mark. I've found that I still have issues today because of this relationship.

I ended up living with him for almost two years, although thinking back, I don't know why I stayed for that long. The final straw came one night after we had gone out to a club together. He had been openly flirting with another girl there, and we fought about it, and I cried and went home by myself. A few hours later, when Craig got home after drinking more, he yelled at me as soon as he walked through the door. I got up out of bed, and he accused me of embarrassing him in front of his friends. He blamed me for what happened!

I yelled back about his flirting with someone else and complained that he didn't respect me. This just made him more angry. He grabbed me, I pulled away, he slapped me, and I fell to the floor. I curled up and cried as he continued yelling, and then I felt a thump on my face and a sharp pain in my eye. He had kicked me. He then stormed out of the room, leaving me alone. I lay there and cried for a little while longer, and then I got up and looked at myself in the bathroom mirror. I had a big black eye.

I cried myself to sleep that night, and Craig slept on the couch. The next day, Craig had already left for work when I got up. Our flatmates didn't even ask about my black eye. I called in sick for work, and I called mum for a talk, she told me to leave Craig. I agreed but wanted to talk to him first. I then packed my bags and waited till he got home.

When he came in, he saw my eye and seemed surprised. He said he hadn't realized he had hurt me and that he was sorry. He also said that he had had too much to drink and made other excuses for his actions. I listened, but my mind was made up. I told him that I had had enough and wanted out of the relationship, as I wasn't happy anymore and couldn't let him hurt me again. He said this wouldn't happen again and pleaded with me to stay, suggesting that I sleep on it before I left. I agreed to stay one more night, but the next day, I took my bags and went back to live with Mum and Gary.

The day after that, Gary came with me to collect the rest of my things from the apartment, and we went while Craig was at work so I didn't have to see him. I haven't seen Craig since, but he did ring me a few times. He apologized and said he wanted me back, but I told him there was no way. I didn't want to see him; it was over.

Chapter 2

New Beginnings

I returned to Mum and Gary's when I was twenty-three, so I commuted from Kogarah to my job in Bondi on public transport, as I hadn't bothered to get my driver's license, and if I couldn't use public transport, someone could always give me a lift. I had been participating in karaoke competitions, and I continued to do these when I could and did really well, either winning or finishing in the top few. I was happy to be single again, but the relationship with Craig had done a lot of damage to my self-confidence and my self-image.

A few months after I broke up with Craig, my friend Danielle, who had recently broken up with my uncle Gary after about four years, asked if I wanted to go on a trip to the Blue Mountains so that she could see Gary again. I agreed, and we headed up to Lawson by train, arriving at Gary's two-bedroom house on Saturday morning. When we arrived, Gary was surprised to see us, as he had just woken up and wasn't aware we were coming to visit. Not long after our arrival, Gary's friend Ian called over as well. Ian was about six feet tall and had curly blonde hair that fell past his shoulders, and he looked to be around my age (it turned out he was actually two years younger than me). I thought he was quite handsome as we all chatted, and I also found him to be outgoing and funny. It was a hot day, so Ian invited us to his house for a swim in his pool. Gary and Danielle spent a lot of time talking to each other, leaving Ian and me to get to know each other. I felt an attraction to Ian, and the more I got to know him, the more I liked him. He liked me as well, and before long, while we were in the pool, we kissed.

Soon after this, Ian and I went on dinner dates and spent time with each other on the weekends. He still seemed really nice and was quite charming. Before long, he asked me to move in with him, and I said yes. We rented a brick house with three bedrooms in Woodford, in the Blue Mountains, where housing was cheap compared to Sydney. I kept my job at Bondi, but the commute from the Blue Mountains was just too long, as it was almost 2 hours each way, so I quit soon after moving. I wasn't sure what my next job would be, but I wanted to do more with my singing career than the karaoke competitions I still entered. I missed living near Mum, but things were going well with Ian, I was happy.

I told Ian that I believed I could see spirits and talk to them, and he thought it was a bit strange, as he didn't really believe in spirits or other supernatural things, but he didn't push his opinions on me. If I believed in spirits, he was okay with that as long as he didn't have to talk to them too!

Although I was generally happy with my life, I felt as if I were missing something, and I wanted a stronger connection with God, so I started going to an Anglican church near our house to see if I could find some of the answers I had been seeking. I did feel the connection with God I wanted, and I enjoyed praying and singing and listening to the services. I also found most other congregants to be friendly, and made a couple of friends there.

Two months after I quit my secretarial job, I saw an ad in the local paper looking for a female singer to join a trio, so I responded. The interview was also an audition, as Ian McLeod, the trio's leader, had me sing for him, and I got the job. I sang with Ian McLeod and the Living Dolls at clubs a couple of times each week and rehearsed with them each week.

I sang with Ian McLeod and the Living Dolls for about four years, and I also sang in the *Johnny O'Keefe Tribute Stage Show*, that McLeod was involved with, which was a great experience, as I got to know some of the other singers Johnny O'Keefe had discovered in the '50s, including Allan Dale, Barry Stanton, Roland Storm, Vicki Forest, and Ralph P. White. A lot of the tribute shows sold out, which made them so exciting. One of the highlights of my time with the show was travelling to Adelaide, where we stayed for six weeks to perform the show in the clubs. I felt like a star! People from the audience wanted my autograph and pictures of me with them. On my time off, I did a lot of sightseeing in Adelaide, which I thought seemed like a well-planned and pretty city.

McLeod was really lovely and supportive and taught me a lot, including how to play the acoustic guitar, and I spent a lot of my spare time practicing. He also encouraged me to write my own songs, and he added music to the lyrics I wrote. He seemed impressed with my writing ability and even had us sing some of my songs at our shows. He also helped me to register these songs with the Australian Performing Rights Association (APRA) so that I'd receive a commission whenever others used them. I still receive a little money from them every few years, so McLeod must still be singing them in shows today.

In subsequent years, I wrote and put music to about one hundred songs of my own, recorded a few on CDs, and made a music video of a song called "On Top of the World," which was played on *Rage*, a popular music show on ABC TV. I also performed and sang as a lead singer in duos after my time with McLeod.

I continued going to church when I could, but I felt that I couldn't completely be myself, as I didn't tell anyone in the congregation about my ability to see and talk to spirits at first. Experience had taught me to hide my abilities, as people's responses had never been good and had always caused me grief. But, after going to church for a few years and making some friends, I finally built up enough courage and trust to talk to some church members about my special gifts, but I decided to talk with the pastor about this first.

I stayed after the church service one afternoon, and when most people had left, I asked the pastor if we could have a talk. He was all smiles and seemed happy to talk to me, so I explained the psychic messages I received and that people who had died came to me to tell me about themselves and asked me to give messages to their loved ones. The pastor's smile faded and he got a very serious, almost angry, look on his face. His responses were cold and uneasy, as if I had brought up a subject that shouldn't be discussed further. He said that I should not talk to the spirits and should try to ignore them, as he believed the psychic messages I received were evil and said that I was playing with fire. "This is the devil's work," he said. "You could go to hell for meddling in such things. You should fear God's wrath."

Being honest paid me no justice again; I was deeply hurt by and angry at his words. The psychic messages I received felt so real and natural, like they were a part of my being deeply ingrained in my soul. And the people who gave me messages were always smiling and so happy to talk to me. I had really started to enjoy their visits and those of the beautiful angels who were also so loving and kind.

I explained to Ian that the pastor had been very judgmental and unaccepting of my ability, and he didn't like that I was upset, so he told me not to go back to that church. He also said a few colourful words about it. His reaction made me feel a little better, I felt safer, and supported, and I stopped going to that church completely.

Ian and I had quite a good relationship for the first few years. During the day, he worked while I relaxed around the house writing songs or reading. I sang at shows around Sydney most weekends, although sometimes I travelled for them, and Ian came to watch me when he could. We did argue at times about many things but, mostly, he yelled and I cried. I felt that Ian lost his temper easily.

Then, at the age of twenty-six, I fell pregnant with my first child. I found out while I was touring with the tribute show in Adelaide and I did a home pregnancy test in my motel room. I was so excited but kept the news a secret till I got home and saw my doctor, as I wanted to be completely sure before I let everyone know. When I did check with my doctor, he confirmed the pregnancy. Ian was also very excited when he found out, but I was a bit scared and worried. In my sixth month, I put my singing career on hold and stopped singing with Ian and the tribute show. I was sad about this and didn't know if I would be able to get back into singing after the birth of my child, but I was determined to be a good mum and had to put the child I was carrying first.

The next few months went by quickly, but as I neared the end, I was so sick of being pregnant and having an aching back. Ian and I moved to a big, old, two-story farmhouse on a hundred acres of land in Little Hartley, near Lithgow. Ian's friends Penny and Chris moved into a smaller house next door. I didn't really like the idea of living out of town but Ian talked me into moving.

On 8 August, at 3:40 a.m., I went into labour, and at 3:40 a.m. on 9 August 1995, Ian and I became the proud parents of a healthy baby boy, Blake. Blake was a beautiful baby, and when I looked into his eyes, I knew he had been on earth before and was an old soul. He looked like a wise old man.

After Blake was born and he and I were released from hospital, Ian took us back to the new house. I had many issues with that house. For one thing, it was far from public transit, and I still didn't have my driver's license, so I was isolated at home with Blake unless Ian was around to drive. We went to the shops once a week and other places only when we needed to, and when Ian was home, he would often walk to his friends' house across the road and stay there for hours.

Being on a property, we often had problems with mice in the house, especially when it rained, even in the kitchen cupboards and once in Blake's cot. I hated the mice and complained about them all the time to Ian, but he told me he couldn't do much to get rid of them.

On top of all of this, there was a spirit in the house that I felt and saw many times. I felt his presence when we first moved in and told Ian about him. He was mostly nice and loved to play with Blake by moving the mobile above his cot and playing with toys, but he could also be grumpy, and I didn't always like his energy. I felt this spirit's presence mostly in the spare room upstairs, which I think was the office when the spirit lived there, and we kept that room empty.

The spirit never gave me his name, but he told me that he had built the house and didn't want to leave. We often heard him moving around, and at times it sounded like he was banging chains on the roof. This frightened me, as he did this when I was by myself in the bedroom.

A week after we moved in, a couple of our friends stayed with us and slept in the spare room. The next day, the lady was totally freaked out and pale. She asked if we were aware of a spirit in the house, especially in the spare room, as he had woken her and showed himself to her, scaring her so much she could hardly move. She also said the room had felt like ice, whereas the other rooms in the house were a normal temperature. Ian and I apologized, as we had known some kind of spiritual presence was there, and we never let anyone sleep in that spare room again.

On one occasion, Nan and my mum and Gary came to visit, and Nan saw the spirit. She described him as a man in an army uniform of about average height and said that he had told her he was Dutch but also spoke English quite well. He showed himself to Nan in the bedroom upstairs not long after she had gone to bed. Nan had seen spirits before, so she just accepted his presence and went off to sleep.

I saw him on a few occasions but was always aware of his presence in the house. He told me he loved Blake, as he and his wife hadn't been able to have any children of their own. He also told me that he had loved his wife very much but had a bad temper that he didn't know how to control. He explained that he suffered from cancer while alive and was slowly wasting away, but he hadn't wanted to be a burden to his wife, so one day, when he was so depressed and in so much pain, he took hold of his shotgun, went to his favourite place on the property, and shot himself dead.

After learning this information, I wrote a song about the spirit:

The Spirit of Hillmeads
(Copyright 1996)

I've never known a love so strong, two people were as one
Their lives were like a fairy-tale, in dreams they'll always belong
Then one day their dream was gone:
He took his life, she was shattered
For nine months in the house all alone, his memory was all that mattered

Chorus

Let your spirit fly like a bird, high into the sky
Soon your soul will be free, for all of eternity

Of everything material they had, the wealth wasn't worth the cost
His love still haunts her broken heart, his spirit in limbo is lost

Repeat chorus

At night she feels his soul, as he wanders and searches for peace

His love and soul are trapped in her mind, now
he is begging her for release

Repeat chorus

I sang to Blake a lot when we were alone in the house, and I also
wrote a song for him:

Song for Blake

Verse 1

Little baby boy, how you sleep so soundly?
I dare not to wake you,
You're a part of me today and forever after,
You are a special gift to me.

Chorus

How I love you!
There's such a bond that I feel,
And God only knows,
He made you just for me.

Verse 2

I look at you as your blue eyes open,
You'll be every girl's dream.
You're a child now, soon you'll be much older,
I'll have these memories to keep

Repeat chorus and verse 1

You are a special gift to me (*repeat*)

Blake was such an adorable baby, and he is now a very clever and lovely young man.

Just before Blake turned one, I had had enough of living in this house. Ian and I had been having more problems since Blake was born and we had moved. I tried to talk to Ian about the fact that I was unhappy, but although he listened, Ian couldn't understand my problems and wouldn't do anything to help. I felt like he didn't care about what I thought.

When I was stuck in the house without much to do, I ruminated about all of the reasons why I was unhappy, which obscured any positive thoughts. I was depressed about where I was living and how I was treated not only by Ian but by people in general. I felt no one respected me and everyone treated me however they wanted to. They made me feel so small and worthless, and they scared me with their aggression. I just couldn't handle my situation.

Ian spent even more time at his friends' place when he wasn't working, and it seemed to me that he was avoiding spending time with me. This may have been because he didn't like listening to me complain. Looking back now, I can see that I often made mountains out of mole hills, but I didn't know how to keep from focusing on what I saw as bad or on what I was unhappy with or how to keep from being negative. I often cried for no real reason, and I felt tired all the time and needed to rest a lot. I talked often on the phone with my mum and told her how I felt. Mum didn't like Ian and thought I would be better off without him.

One day, when Blake was around eleven months old, while Ian was at work, I asked my stepdad, Gary, to hire a truck to pick up my furniture and belongings from Little Hartley. Gary arrived a couple of hours later, and we packed up what we could, and I left the house and Ian. I was excited to leave, but also scared, as I still loved Ian. I had asked him on many occasions to move back to Lawson so I could be closer to the shops and public transport, but he wouldn't move, so I felt I had no other choice than to leave him. This was such a hard choice to make, but I couldn't stand living on that property anymore and felt that if I stayed there I would go insane.

Mum and Gary were living in a small flat in Penrith that didn't have a lot of room for us all of us, so Mum, Gary, Blake, and I moved to the Central Coast to start a new life. We stayed in a caravan park for a few weeks, and while there, I got food poisoning, which took a heavy toll on my health. Finally, we found a house to rent in Woy Woy across the road from the railway station and not too far from the shopping centre to walk there, as mum also didn't drive. We stayed at this house for about six months. Mum and Gary loved having me with them, and they helped me look after Blake and spoiled him. I went onto a single-parent pension and didn't work besides housework.

Ian was angry with me when I first left. I took him to court and received full custody of Blake, but Ian had visitation rights. At first he picked Blake up at Gosford Police Station, but then I took Blake to a day-care centre in Gosford so I could drop him off and the staff could hand him to Ian, which made me a lot more comfortable, as I didn't have to see Ian then. Ian moved back to Lawson a few months after I left.

After I moved, I was feeling lost inside and I wanted to find a deeper connection with God, so I started going to a Pentecostal church near Umina Beach, about ten minutes from Woy Woy. I really enjoyed it there and a met a nice couple, Bronwyn and

Shane, who gave me lifts to and from church. I got to sing on stage with the band a couple of times, and I really enjoyed this. I also joined a prayer group and went to Bible study. About six months after I started going to this church, Bronwyn and Shane asked me if I wanted to become baptized. I agreed and was baptized the following weekend at Umina Beach.

Soon, Mum, Gary, and I decided to move to another house, as living near the railway line at Woy Woy was very noisy, and we found a newly painted two-bedroom villa with a pretty courtyard out the back in Point Claire. Blake and I loved it there, and Blake could play and splash in his plastic shell paddling pool outside in the courtyard.

Blake got ear infections regularly once we moved to the Central Coast, and after about six months, Blake got such a bad ear that he needed to be hospitalized. The doctors said that he needed an operation to put grommets into Blake's inner ear and explained the risks: Blake could lose his hearing in the right ear, as it had swelled to be three times bigger than his left ear, and any operation had a chance of complications.

I was really worried on the night before the operation, but as I slept in a hospital bed with Blake, I had a vivid dream in which a huge male angel with deep blue eyes came to visit me. He told me that his name was Michael and that he was here to protect Blake, so I shouldn't worry. He reassured me that the operation would go smoothly and that Blake would make a full recovery.

When I woke shortly after the dream, I saw a glow of light above Blake, I looked around to see if anyone else was in the room, but the nurses on duty were in the nurses' station around the corner, and everyone else I could see was asleep. I looked back at

Blake, and the light was gone. Blake was sleeping soundly, but I whispered to him about my dream before I went back to sleep myself. When I woke up the next morning, I felt much more relaxed about the operation.

Mum and Gary arrived shortly after I was up and sat with me during the operation. I told them about my dream, and they both said that they hoped I was right, but I could tell that they were still worried. I was used to this reaction, and I knew Blake would be fine. After the operation, the doctor came out to see us and told us that everything had gone well and that Blake should make a full recovery. Blake stayed in the hospital for one more day, but as he recovered so well, the doctor let me take him home after that.

When we moved to Point Claire, I stopped going to the Pentecostal church, as it was too hard to get to, but a couple of weeks after Blake had recovered, I saw a notice in the local paper about a Christian singles' group that met up most weekends around my area, so I decided to go. I met them at a lovely bush land setting with cascading waterfalls in Peats Ridge, on a hot, sunny day. Not long after I arrived, I started a conversation with a man called Jonathon who I found handsome. He said he was in his early thirties, and he seemed gentle and sensitive. We hit it off straight away and found out we had a lot of interests in common. He had been separated from his wife for about a year and had a son the same age as Blake. We spent the whole day laughing and chatting and occasionally going for dips under the waterfalls. Jonathon and I exchanged phone numbers just before we left and talked about meeting up in the next few days. I was so excited. I really liked him and couldn't wait to see him again.

After that, Jonathon and I saw each other quite regularly. He picked me up to go to the beach, on bushwalks, to dinner and movies, and so on. I then started going to Niagara Park Baptist Church, which was connected to the singles' group and the church Jonathon attended, so we went to services together. After we had been going out for a few months, Blake and I moved in with Jonathon, who owned his own home in Kariong, on the Central Coast.

Around this time, Nan decided to sell the house she lived in alone in Penrith to move closer to Mum, as her health had become an issue, and to escape the very cold winters and very hot summers. Mum and Gary moved out of their villa and into a townhouse in Point Claire, with Nan living downstairs and Mum and Gary living upstairs.

I had been living with Jonathon for over seven months, but this turned out to not be what I was hoping for, as he also suffered from depression himself. I often found him sitting with his head in his hands. I was totally unable to help Jonathan with his issues, as I had enough of my own to deal with. He had a good connection with his son, Justin, but didn't form a close bond with Blake, and this was easily evident as he didn't interact much with Blake at all. Jonathon's father lived on a farm near Peats Ridge, and we sometimes visited him, but he was verbally abusive, putting Jonathan down all the time. I didn't like how he treated Jonathon and didn't like going there.

Blake's immune system was quite weak, and he picked up bugs easily, so he was often sick. A stomach condition put him in isolation in the hospital for a week. His belly swelled, and he was a very sick little boy. Jonathan didn't seem to really care at all and gave me no support. He wasn't interested in Blakes condition and didn't come to visit him.

After living with Jonathan for about eight months, I decided to leave him and talked to my mum about moving in with her, Gary, and Nan, but the townhouse was too small, and the block of units didn't allow children to live there, as most of the residents were elderly. Mum suggested that I talk to Ian's mother, Maurine, whom I had been seeing about once a month since I moved to the Coast. She came to visit Blake, and we spent the day together talking and playing with Blake. Maurine was a lovely lady and always understanding and supportive of me, so I contacted her and told her about my situation. She suggested that I live with her until I had sorted out what I wanted to do, so Blake and I moved back to Lawson and in with her for a while.

A few weeks later, Maurine asked if Ian could come to see Blake, and I said that was fine, so Ian arrived shortly afterwards. As he played with Blake, I saw the connection between them and the love in Ian's eyes. I was impressed with Ian, as he was nice to me, and after we talked a little, he seemed to have gotten his act together.

In the following weeks, Ian came over to see Blake more and more often, and I also went over to Ian's with Blake. I was still mixed up about my feelings for Ian, but I felt a lot more comfortable with him, and we got on great again. One thing led to another, and before long, we had decided to give it another go, and I moved back in with him, to the house he rented not far from his mother's.

I was hopeful that things would be different this time. I wanted to get my driver's license and a car. I first got my L plates and began driving lessons, and then I shopped for cars. I told Ian I didn't want anything fancy, but he organized a loan and bought me a brand-new burgundy Ford Falcon. I was overwhelmed but excited. Before long, I got my provisional license. Being able to drive gave me a real sense of freedom, and it was great not having to rely on public transport anymore. I wished I had got my license when I was younger, but better late than never.

One night a couple of months after Blake and I moved in with Ian, when I was sleeping, I felt a heavy pressure on my body like some negative force was holding me down and trying to suffocate me. I woke up shaking, and when I told Ian, he thought it may have been a bad dream. A few days later, when I was in between waking and sleep, I heard a dark and eerie voice calling Blake's name. I instantly woke up wondering what was going on, and later, Blake said he saw scary yellow eyes looking at him through the window that night. I knew then that the house had a negative spirit or force attached to it. On many occasions after this, I felt as though I had been psychically attacked and like someone or something was watching me, and it wasn't nice.

I had been going to a new church since I had moved back to Lawson, and I told some of my new acquaintances about what I was experiencing, and they offered to come over to cleanse the house. To do so, they walked through the house chanting prayers, and after this, the negative spirit was gone and the energy of the house was much more peaceful. I later found out that the people who had lived in the house before had been into voodoo and dark magic.

About six weeks after this, I found out that I was pregnant with my second child, and Ian was thrilled. We decided to get married, set a date close enough that I wouldn't look pregnant in our wedding photos, and started making arrangements.

The first few months of the pregnancy, I had bad morning sickness and even vomited blood. I also suffered depression and cried a lot.

I felt like I couldn't talk to anyone about how I was feeling, and I found it hard being away from my mum, as she still lived on the Central Coast, three hours away by car, so I didn't get to see her much. I missed having her help too, as I found it hard to cope with Blake on my own while Ian worked long hours. I told my doctor about my feelings, and she put me on antidepressants and arranged for a nurse to call in each week to check on me. The nurse, a lovely lady named Arwin, would check my blood pressure and talk to me about how I was coping. We talked about other things as well, and she mentioned that she did palm readings, so I asked her to look at my hand and see what she could tell me.

I was intrigued by how accurate her reading just of my palm was about my life up to that point. After this, I bought a book about palmistry and read it over and over, trying to memorize as much as I could, and when I had, I bought another book about palmistry and did the same again, as even though both books covered much of the same information, the second explained it differently. I really studied, and I practised on myself and my friends, but I didn't have the courage to do an actual palm reading for anyone else.

Around this time, I met a woman who invited me to attend a spiritualist church in Springwood that she went to. It wasn't far away, and services were held in a small hall once a month for about thirty people. I really enjoyed the church, as everyone was so nice and made me feel welcome, and I also really enjoyed the service, as the speakers talked about spirits openly and did healing energy work, something like reiki, for those who wanted it. We sang songs and talked about God and angels, and then someone did spiritual readings. I connected deeply with this church's beliefs, and I went to as many services as I could after that.

During one service, a medium doing readings on the platform came up to me and brought through the spirit of my uncle Terry. The medium described him in great detail, and I was overwhelmed with emotion, as I had been close to Terry. She then told me things that no one else could have known. For example, I had contemplated committing suicide around this time, and the medium said, "Terry is telling me to tell you not to do what he did. You have so much to live for; it's not worth it. You will only have to come back again in another life and repeat the same lessons that you didn't understand." I couldn't believe what I was hearing; my mind swirled and a wave of emotion came over me. The words hit home and rang so true to me that I started crying uncontrollably. To know Terry was with me was such a great source of comfort and strength. I felt like a weight had been lifted off my shoulders, as anytime thoughts of suicide popped into my head, I thought about what Terry had said through the medium that day. That message changed my perspective on life.

In June 1999, Ian and I were married in a lovely park in Lawson before a few friends and family members. It was a beautiful day, and everything went smoothly. I was about four months pregnant by then, but my wedding dress hid it well. Ian and I didn't have enough money for a honeymoon, so we just went home after the reception.

Then, on the 19th November 1999, after a three-hour labour, I gave birth to our second child, Jacob.

Although Ian and I were generally okay, we were having problems with money: we didn't have enough coming in, and we fell behind on payments. Creditors hassled Ian about money he owed for his painting and decorating business and that we owed on bills. Ian put in long hours at work and came home tired and grumpy quite often. He helped around the house a little, but he felt that because he worked so much, I should do most of the housework. He had always been great with the Blake and played with him often, and he even helped care for Jacob a little, feeding him or changing his nappy, but most of the time he was either at work or too tired. We argued a lot about money, the children, and the housework.

I still went to the spiritualist church as often as I could, and as I got to know some people there, I opened up to them about my experiences with angels and spirits. They were thrilled and asked if I had ever done readings. I told them I had been studying palmistry but had never practised it on anyone, so they asked if I could have a look at their palms. I was a bit scared about this, as I had never tested my skills in this way, but I felt comfortable with these people, and they put no real pressure on me, saying that I could just see how it went and that it didn't matter if I didn't pick up much.

I looked at a woman's palm and told her what the lines on her palm and fingers said to me, and while I was holding her hand, I also picked up on other information about her. I told her about this, and all the ladies were amazed and asked how I could know this information from reading a palm. I said that it had just popped into my head. This also impressed them, and I continued the reading for another fifteen minutes and then performed a reading for another woman that went similarly. This was the first time I did psychic readings for anyone.

After this, members of the church asked me to do readings regularly. I held their hands to look at their palms, but more and more often, images flashed through my mind or thoughts popped into my head about the person whose palm I was reading. Names of people both living and in spirit connected to the person came to me, and I felt emotions and physical sensations in my body that related to the spirit. I never charged any money for these readings, and I performed them almost every month for the two years that I attended this church. The other members thought I was a gifted psychic, but I still didn't really see myself as a psychic or as a medium, as reading for others was so new to me still and I lacked self-confidence.

I felt drawn to learning more about spirituality, so I read more books on spiritual and religious topics and listened intently to the talks at church meetings. The more I learnt, the better I understood many topics, and I deepened my connection with God, spirits and myself. I enjoyed meditating at the meetings and was able to talk openly to anyone about spiritual topics.

About fourteen months after I had Jacob, I fell pregnant again. I was a bit shocked, but I was happy that Blake and Jacob would have another brother or sister. I still suffered from depression, however, and found this pregnancy hard, as I didn't have the emotional help I needed and even though I was on antidepressants. Ian supported me the best he could, and I saw a counsellor once a week to learn how to cope with my emotions, and these did help a little, but my anxiety remained, and so did my negative thoughts about myself and my life.

Ian and I had moved houses a couple of times by now. The house we had been renting when we first got back together was old, so we moved into a nicer and newer house after Jacob was born, but after we lived there for almost a year, the house was sold and we had to move again.

Ian talked to his mother about our housing situation because he wanted to buy a house in hopes that it would give me more stability and help my depression and that it would give our relationship more stability too. After some thought, Maurine gave Ian the money for a deposit on a home. He and I were excited and found a nice but old home only a few blocks from Maurine's place. We moved in when I was about six months pregnant.

The house was rundown, so Ian wasted no time in fixing it up, and he spent many of his days off renovating and painting. However, the work seemed to take ages because he didn't have much spare time to do it in and we didn't have much money to spend. Owning our own house did make me feel more secure, as it was great knowing that we wouldn't have to move again, but my depression and other issues continued, so I was never completely happy.

When I had my ultrasound, I decided to find out the sex of the baby and learnt that it was a little girl. I was so excited! I loved my boys, but to have a little girl is what a mum dreams of. Each night I confided in my spirit guides and prayed to God and the angels to help me have a quick labour and for my baby girl to be healthy. I also prayed for my baby to be born during the day, as both the boys were born around 3:00 a.m., and for her to be born on the day she was due, as both the boys had been overdue.

This pregnancy was much better than my last, as I didn't suffer from morning sickness as I had with Jacob, but as my due date approached, I was so looking forward to not being pregnant anymore. The night before my due date, I had a very vivid dream in which six pairs of angel eyes hovered over my bed, and the angels said, "Your baby will be born on her due date. You will have her in the daytime, and you will have a quick labour." They repeated these words for what seemed like ten or fifteen minutes.

The next morning, on the 1ˢᵗ December 2001 at about 7:00, my waters broke. Ian quickly took me to the hospital, and one hour later, I gave birth to Shaylee-Jade. Everything I had prayed for and that the angels said would happen came true. My newborn girl was truly heaven-sent. I was so happy to have a little girl, and I decided that three children were enough. I talked to Ian about this and then organized to have my tubes tied.

Ian continued working a lot and leaving me to take care of the house and kids, and our money problems continued. I had to shop at second-hand stores, and we needed food stamps. Ian worked hard and did his best, but his schedule left him tired and irritable. I didn't make it any easier for him. Ian took out his frustration with little things, such as the house not being clean enough or his dinner not being ready, out on me.

My three young children were a real handful. Each was very demanding, and they sapped my energy. I had trouble keeping up with them and needed more rest. I tried to talk to Ian about these issues, but he didn't understand how to help me, and I unloaded my troubles and worries onto my mother over the phone, and she seemed to understand, but she lived too far away to help more than emotionally.

As an only child, I had received a lot of attention from Mum, but looking back, I see that she may have protected me too much, as I didn't learn how to cope with difficulties. Mum was such an influence on me that when she looked at something negatively, then I saw it that way too. I love my mum with all of my heart, and I know she did her best raising me, and in many ways she did a great job. I always tried to make my mum happy, as I didn't like it when she got upset with me. In fact, I didn't like confrontation in general or when people raised their voices and put out any negative energy. I hid from others when I felt upset or scared or anxious, and I passively went along with what other people wanted to avoid conflict. I was afraid to voice my own opinion, and I felt it didn't matter and that I didn't matter.

The headaches I had regularly turned into migraines, and my depression worsened to the point that I didn't want to get out of bed some days, and if I absolutely had to, I'd get up but then go back to bed straight away. I cried often for no real reason. Everything was just too much. I didn't like where my life was, and I didn't like where it was heading.

Not long after Shaylee was born, Ian and I had an argument in the kitchen. His yelling at me made me feel so small, like I was a bad mother because I couldn't keep up with the work I was expected to do, and I felt guilty for not being good enough. I cried uncontrollably. Then I just collapsed, my muscles twitching uncontrollably as though I were experiencing an epileptic fit.

Ian carried me into the bedroom and put me on the bed, and I passed out. When I came to a short time later, I was groggy and my muscles felt like jelly. I couldn't stand and couldn't talk, and I was confused and afraid. I didn't remember passing out and didn't know why I couldn't get up or talk. When I tried to answer Ian, who was talking to me, I could only make sounds and say, "I." Ian then picked me up and carried me out to the car, and he grabbed the kids and drove them to his mum's and then took me to the hospital.

When we arrived, a nurse put me in a wheelchair and took me into the emergency department. A doctor then gave me a quick examination and said I had experienced a nervous breakdown. He gave me some medication kept me in hospital for only a few hours for observation and didn't run any tests. The doctor said I may feel a little weak for a while and advised me to take it easy. Ian then took me home, but I still felt like a zombie. I had a lot of trouble just getting to my feet, and then I couldn't walk properly, as my legs still felt like jelly. I also had trouble maintaining my grip on things and dropped them easily. I couldn't even hold my cutlery and had trouble eating. My speech was also slurred, and I still couldn't put thoughts into words. This made it almost impossible for me to take care of the children and do the housework.

The next day, Ian called my mother to tell her what had happened. He asked her to stay with us for a while to help me, but Mum hated Ian by this point, as they had clashed many times, and although she loved me and wanted to help, she was not prepared to stay in the house with Ian, and she didn't come. She also had no transport to our house, so it wasn't like she could just pop in. Anyway, if she had come, I knew it would only have caused more trouble between them, as she wouldn't put up with any crap.

Over the following weeks and months, Ian had to take a lot of time off work to look after me and the children. I visited my doctor regularly after my breakdown, and she said that what I had experienced had all of the symptoms of being a minor stroke combined with a mental breakdown, so she organized some appointments with a psychologist and referred me to a neurologist at Katoomba Hospital, the neurologist said that I was lucky to be alive, and she seemed angry that the doctors at the hospital had sent me home without doing any scans to check if I had had a stroke.

In the months that followed, Ian's mother, Maurine, popped in to help look after the children and me when Ian had to work. She sometimes got frustrated with me and said on a number of occasions that I needed to toughen up, as I was too sensitive. She was really a lovely lady, but she didn't understand me and what I was going through. Then, Ian and I fell behind on the payments for my car, and it was repossessed, which made it very hard for us to get places, although Maurine lent us her car at times so that we could get around.

My health gradually improved, but it took me six months to get most of my strength back and to walk and talk properly again. As I recovered, my spirit guides told me that I could stay with Ian and die or could leave and live. I wasn't happy in my relationship and hadn't been happy for a while, and I didn't want to stay and die, so I packed my belongings, grabbed the kids, loaded up the car, and left Ian.

I went to the Central Coast, but there wasn't enough room for me and all the kids in my mum's unit, so I rang up the Salvation Army, which organized for us to stay at a nearby women's refuge. When I arrived there, I told them my story and that my kids and I needed somewhere to sleep, and they were happy to accept me. We stayed there for three weeks, during time at the shelter, I had to give Maurine's car back, which left me without a car and once again reliant on public transport. I brought a letter from my doctor explaining my condition to Centrelink and arranged to go on a disability pension, and I agreed with Ian that he could have the children on weekends. I also regularly saw my mother. We met at the waterfront park near her house, and we played with the kids. I soon found a house near Toukley. I was so glad to leave the shelter, as a woman who came to stay a few days after I arrived was verbally abusive to me and made my situation worse.

A few months after we moved to Toukley, I met a man who was selling an old green car for five hundred dollars, and as I didn't have a car at the time, I bought it. I was so happy to be able to drive wherever I needed to go again. I had enrolled Blake into a primary school, so I was now able to drive him to and from school, but after about two weeks of the school run, the car broke down in a no-stopping zone across from the school. Cars beeped at me, as their drivers didn't realize I had broken down, and I was stressed. About five minutes later, a man stopped, got out of his car, and helped me. He said his name was Wayne and that he was a mechanic, and he fixed the problem with the car, and we got talking and found out we were both single parents in our early thirties, and that he had a son one year older than Blake at the same school. We exchanged phone numbers and then said our goodbyes. A few days later, we met up at a beach near Toukley. I found him to be a nice man, and we got on well and had some things in common, so we dated more after that.

Not long after meeting Wayne, I had another small breakdown. The kids fought and screamed at each other over the smallest of things, and I just couldn't handle them. It caused me so much stress that on this occasion when the kids just would not listen to me at all, I collapsed. I tried to talk to Blake, but my words were slurred, and I couldn't put thoughts together. Blake called my mum and Gary and told them what had happened. They came straight over and took me to the doctor's.

The doctor told me that the strain of taking care of the children was just too much for me and that if I chose to continue looking after them, I would most likely have a complete breakdown, which could kill me. Mum suggested that the kids could live with their father until they were a bit older and I was stronger.

I had a talk with Ian about this, and I learnt that he had begun living with a woman called Fiona, who was home while Ian was at work, and they agreed to take the children during the week, leaving them with me at the weekends. Ian was very supportive of this decision, which helped immensely, and we continued this arrangement for about two years.

When the kids left, I felt a deep loss, even though I knew I wasn't capable of looking after them at that time. Many days I sat on my own and cried because I missed them deeply. I felt like I was spiralling downwards again and wondered if life was worth living anymore. I thought I had done the right thing by leaving Ian, but no matter which way I turned, I hit emotional obstacles. The psychologist and counsellors I would see offered little help, I felt out of control and didn't know who to turn to. I suffered panic attacks on multiple occasions before I picked up the children, as I worried about their arguing and about how I would cope with them. I felt like I was hanging on by a thread that could break at any time. I didn't have the awareness or the necessary tools at that time to know any different.

A few weeks after the children left, I moved into a two-bedroom flat a few minutes from the beach. I started to recover, and I enjoyed my time with the kids when they stayed with me. My mother and stepfather, who lived just across the road, often took Blake overnight while Jacob and Shaylee slept at my flat. This made it easier for me to cope, as it reduced the kids' fighting. I was blessed to have Mum and Gary's love and protection.

When the kids weren't with me, I had more time to focus on myself. I tried to get my singing career going again by going to karaoke and entering singing competitions that I often won. Through these I met a man called Dave, who was a singer and musician, and we formed a duo called Evolution. He got us gigs at clubs and performing at private functions such as weddings. We recorded a CD and sent it to some agents, and although we didn't have much luck, singing with Dave was lots of fun and helped me start to rebuild my confidence.

During this time on my own, I also began attending spiritualist churches on the Central Coast, where I met some lovely people and made some friends, and I also joined a meditation group and met with them once a week at a lady's home in Tuggerah. At the end of each meditation session, members of the group took turns doing psychic readings for each other. We wrote down everything we picked up, and I always wrote a lot more than anybody else in the group. Before long, I received more accurate psychic information from the spirits more often, some of the group members encouraged me to do paid readings. They all thought that I was a wonderful psychic, and this gave me confidence in my ability.

My new friends suggested that I put my name down at a few cafe's where other psychics did readings, and once or twice a week, I sat at the cafes and did readings for those who approached me. I usually picked up two or three readings in a day and charged twenty-five dollars per reading, from which the shop took a five-dollar cut. On a good week, I could make around one hundred dollars, but other weeks I earned only forty dollars or no money at all.

I would get very anxious before readings, worrying whether I would pick up any information and whether a client would be happy with the readings. I gave clients at least an hour to make sure they got their money's worth, and some of the people told me that they really enjoyed their readings and that I was very good, but others just said thanks and went on their way. None of my clients said they were unhappy with what I picked up, but if they even suggested that they were a little disappointed or that they were hoping for something more specific, this shattered my confidence and kept me from wanting to do readings for a while.

The little I earned was a big help to supplement my pension, although I still often needed to go to charity places to get food stamps and vouchers to help with the electricity and phone bills. The Salvation Army had given me some furniture and bedding for the kids, which was also a great help. What spare money I had after paying for rent and petrol went to clothes for the kids bought from second-hand stores. When the car had gearbox trouble and broke down, I couldn't afford to have it fixed, so I had to borrow Wayne's car or rely on public transport.

I had started going to the gym to build up my strength and really enjoyed it and had a lot more energy and was fit and slim. Exercise also helped me recover from the breakdowns and the stroke as it balanced me and helped me to focus my mind. I went to the gym four or five times a week, as besides being a saviour for me as well, it was a positive activity that made me happy.

I also loved spending hours on the beach sunbaking and swimming. I found the water therapeutic, and being at the beach was better than sitting at home feeling sorry for myself.

Wayne then asked me to move in with him, and I did for about ten months, but this arrangement didn't work out very well. Wayne didn't have a lot of patience when my kids were with me, and he got very angry with them at times, and Wayne's son, Joey, who was quite spoilt, lived with us full-time. He got angry if my kids even went near any of his belongings and bullied my kids, and they often complained to me about him. Given these problems, I decided it was best that I move out, although Wayne and I didn't break up.

We continued to see each other a few times each week, but I didn't love him. It just felt comfortable and safe for him to be there, and I felt that I needed Wayne's support.

I couldn't seem to find what I was looking for in a man: someone who would really take care of me, was understanding, who treated my kids and me with respect. I wanted someone with compassion, who was strong but gentle, and it would have also been great if they could cook. I had a much clearer picture of what I didn't want: someone who was aggressive and who wasn't a big drinker, as Wayne could be, I needed someone sensitive.

Despite my slim figure from working out and good looks, my self-image issues continued, and so did my depression. I was sometimes scared of having my kids because of their fighting and demands, and I hated the long trip to pick them up and take them back. The car was like a war zone with their yelling and hitting. Jacob was now five, and the most difficult to handle at that time, he seemed to be the one starting the fights. Blake was nine, he tried to help me, and I felt that he was trying to take on the role of a father figure, but Jacob hated this treatment, and it made his behaviour worse.

When my gym membership was due, I didn't have the money to renew it, so I had to let this pleasure slide for a while. I continued to pursue my music career. I always believed that I would be famous one day, this belief gave me an inner drive. This determination and persistence as I followed my dreams had always been a positive trait. The duo with Dave had fizzled out, as we hadn't had much work, but I made my own recording of some of the songs I had written to send to recording companies in hopes that I'd get discovered and land a contract.

I felt something in my life had to change, but I didn't know how to bring that about I felt something missing, and I was full of self-doubt, lacked confidence, and suffered from debilitating emotional issues. My migraine headaches sometimes lasted for days, and my depression was often intense. I considered suicide many times, as I didn't believe I was a good mother, my relationships had all fallen apart, and I never seemed to have enough money.

Over the two years since I had moved to the coast, I did feel happy at times, but the times when I was not happy greatly outnumbered them. Life was a struggle no matter what I did.

Chapter 3

Finding True Love

This is where my story truly begins, everything began to change, and it's continued to get better since. This is my real-life fairy tale of how I come to meet my knight in shining armour!

Late in the afternoon on Friday, 11 March 2005, when I was thirty-six years old, I was doing some shopping at Coles supermarket at the Entrance and had a few items in my trolley when I turned into the stationery aisle, which was empty except for one person, whom I recognized straight away as a woman named Joan.

I knew Joan, a lovely woman in her late fifties who practised reiki, from the spiritualist church and the meditation group I attended. She looked up, and I said hello.

She had a big smile on her face said, "Oh, hi, Suzie! I've been wanting to run into you for a while now. I have something to tell you." As she said these words, a couple of packets of envelopes fell off a shelf near us and scattered across the floor. Neither of us had touched the shelf, so we both looked around but didn't see anyone else near us.

"Wow, isn't that strange?" I said.

"Yes," she responded.

"I think this is a sign. What did you want to tell me?"

"There's a shop at Long Jetty that's looking for psychics to do readings. I thought it might interest you."

It did interest me. I looked again at all of the envelopes on the floor and felt again that this was really important. I asked her for the name of the shop, and she said it was called Little Arrows Romantic Gifts and that it was run by a nice man and his parents, who helped out while he was working at his other job as a chef. Joan explained that she had been doing reiki treatments in a back room and running a meditation class in a back room and that a couple of other ladies did tarot card readings, but the owner was really hoping to find a medium like myself to do readings as well.

I felt more strongly that this message was important and had no doubt that the envelopes had been pushed from the shelf by spirit. This was big. I had goosebumps, and cold shivers ran down my spine. I thanked Joan and told her I was going to the shop straight away! She said that there was no hurry and that I could call in the next time I went past, but I said, "No. I am going now." I then left my shopping trolley in the aisle and started to leave.

"What about your shopping?" Joan called behind me.

"It will be here when I come back," I said and left.

I arrived at the shop shortly after. The front of the shop was painted bright yellow with rainbows, butterflies, and angels, and two trees in pots shaped into hearts stood at each side of the entrance. Inside, the walls were bright green, red, blue, pink, and orange, and the shelves contained statues and figurines, ornaments, trinkets, novelty gifts, books on love and spirituality, candles, incense, toiletries, cards, flowers, and balloons. The shop also sold jewellery and crystals, paintings, plaques, and poetry. It smelt beautiful and it looked like a happy place.

A bright older lady behind the counter welcomed me into the shop and asked how she could help me. I told her that I had heard they were looking for a psychic and that I hoped I could do readings there. The woman said her name was Pat, and we had a lovely talk. I learnt that her son Stephen owned the business and that I would need to talk to him but that he was currently at his restaurant job in Terrigal and wouldn't be back until late that evening. She felt sure that he would be happy to have me do readings at the shop, as he wanted to add more psychics. She then introduced me to her husband, Arthur, who was out the back, and gave me a tour.

Pat told me quite a lot about how Stephen had come to have the shop and how she and Arthur had come to help him. Before I knew it, more than half an hour had gone and the shop was about to close. I told Pat that I would come back over the weekend to talk to Stephen. I said goodbye, and she said, "Bye! Welcome to the family!"

What a strange thing to say, I thought. I knew that she meant to welcome me to the family business, but it still felt a bit unusual. I then went back to the supermarket. I found my trolley where I had left it, and with everything in it, so I finished shopping and headed back to my flat.

The following Sunday afternoon, 13 March 2005, I went to the beach with my kids and then left at 3:00 so that I could call into the shop to meet the owner. I took the kids to my mother's and asked her to watch them for a little while, said I shouldn't be too long, and then drove the five minutes to Little Arrows Romantic Gifts, arriving at about 3:30 and still wearing my bikini and a sarong wrapped around my waist.

When I walked into the shop, I saw a man behind the counter who looked to be around my age and was well over six feet tall, slim, and handsome. I introduced myself and explained that I had been in a couple of days ago and had spoken with his mother. He asked me if I was the poet, as apparently another woman with blonde hair who was a poet had been in talking to his mother, and Stephen said he was a poet as well. I said that I was a psychic, and he told me that his mother had told him about me as well.

We discussed my doing readings and worked out which days I would be available, and I gave him my contact details and got an introduction to the shop and learnt about the other psychics who did readings there. I knew one of them from the church I attended.

Stephen then invited me to the meditation classes, and we talked about meditation and spirituality. He also talked about his children and his past, I talked about my life too, and we just kept talking for what seemed like no time at all, but by then it was already after 5:00 and he had to close the shop and head off to work at the restaurant. I left the shop at 5:20, and Stephen still had to lock up. I learnt later he was fifteen minutes late for his shift that night.

I had a big smile on my face. I was happy that I would be working there and would hopefully earn a little extra money. I felt so comfortable talking to Stephen. He seemed so wise and knowledgeable about spirituality. I was at ease talking to him about personal details from my past, and I remember admiring how Stephen had gone through a lot and was so understanding. We had a lot in common, and I was attracted to him.

I headed back to Mum's to get the kids, and when I arrived, Mum was wondering what had taken so long, as I had to drop off the kids with Ian in Sydney at 7:00 and was going to be late. I hurried back to my flat, called Ian to let him know I was running late, and then headed off with the kids.

The following Tuesday evening, I went to the meditation group at the shop. Stephen, Pat, Joan, and five other people were there. The meditation went for thirty minutes, and then we had coffee, tea, and homemade biscuits and scones. I got to know everyone and also talked with Stephen a little more.

Then, the next Saturday, Stephen called me to say that two ladies, sisters, wanted a combined reading from me. I told him that was okay and that I could be there in thirty minutes, as I had to take my kids over to my mum's. He started to tell me what he knew about these sisters, but I cut him off.

"Don't tell me anything about them," I said. "I would prefer not to know anything before I do their reading."

He apologized and said he would see me soon.

Stephen greeted me when I arrived and took me up the side path to the back room, where I set up for the reading, and about ten minutes later, he brought the sisters in. I remember the reading well. One of the sisters had a little boy who was terminally ill and didn't have much time left. Both of the sisters were upset, but the child's mother was finding it particularly hard to cope with the pending loss. I talked to them about what happens when we die and told them about the angels that came to them. The sisters' grandparents also came through in spirit with lots of information.

The reading lasted a little over ninety minutes, and when they left, they said they felt much more at peace and more positive about the future. I had really impressed them with what I picked up from spirit. The sisters came back to see me a few months later after the boy had passed away so that they could connect with him, and that was a beautiful reading.

After the reading, Stephen wanted to introduce me to his son and daughter. Unfortunately, I had to go pick up my kids and didn't have time, so he arranged to see me at the meditation the following Tuesday.

I had only met Stephen a couple of times and we had only talked, but something had already formed between us. I could feel that he was attracted to me, and I was attracted to him, but I was unsure about him. I had only just met him, so nothing could happen between us yet. Still, we had something, but I had no idea what it was. I felt excited but didn't know why. Little did I know that my whole life was about to change.

I arrived at Stephen's shop for the meditation class at 7:00 p.m. on Tuesday. I thought I was early, as only Joan, who ran the group, and Pat and Stephen were there. They told me that this was strange, as at least six people came each week, but it was the week before the Easter holidays. We went ahead and did the meditation, which was lovely, and then Joan and Pat went off to make the coffee and tea, leaving me alone with Stephen.

He leaned towards me and said softly that he had been hoping to get me alone with him tonight, as he wanted to ask me out on a date if I were interested. I was surprised that he had asked me out so soon. I think I just responded, "Oh."

He continued, saying that he had been thinking that on the following Thursday evening, we could go to a nice restaurant. I was still in shock, and a thousand things went through my mind. *Thursday night? I am supposed to pick up my kids, and Friday is Good Friday, so I have to get them on Thursday. I have to break up with Wayne, and then I won't have a car.* I sat there for a few seconds, and then I said, "I can't on Thursday."

Stephen was like, "Oh, okay. I understand. Sorry."

I could see on his face that he was disappointed, so I said straight away, "It's just that I'm supposed to pick up my kids on Thursday night in Sydney. I could do another night, say, next week?"

He smiled, and we set a date for the Thursday after Easter. Then Pat and Joan came back into the room with the tea and coffee, and we chatted for a few minutes, and then I got ready to leave. I gave everyone a goodnight cuddle, and Stephen made sure he got a little cuddle from me as well.

The next morning after breakfast, I called Ian, explaining that I was going to break up with Wayne and so couldn't use his car anymore. I didn't know how I was going to be able to pick up and drop off the children each week and wasn't sure what to do. Ian was very understanding and wanted to help me, and he said he had a friend who was selling his car. He offered to buy it for me and drive it to The Entrance on Friday with the kids. I was over overwhelmed with gratitude and thanked him. I couldn't believe it. I asked if his partner, Fiona, would be okay with that, but he told me not to worry about that, as he would explain it to her.

I then went over to see Wayne at work. I told him that I just wasn't happy in the relationship, didn't love him, and wanted to stop seeing him. He was a bit upset, but this wasn't the first time I had told him this, so I'm not sure if he took me seriously. But then I gave him his car keys and told him where I had parked. I didn't stay very long and caught a bus back home.

When I got back to my flat I called Little Arrows to let Stephen know that my plans had changed and that I was free on Thursday night after all. I spoke to Pat, who said he was working that night but that she would let him know I called and would pass on my message.

The next morning, Stephen called me back. I explained my new schedule and asked if he might still want to go out this week. He did and he thanked me for letting him know. I gave him my address and directions to my flat, and he told me he would pick me up at about 6:15 that evening for dinner at a local restaurant.

I had butterflies in my stomach all day, combined with an upset stomach from a mild dose of food poisoning that I was still getting over. I tried to relax at the beach until it was time to go home to get ready. I picked out an apricot dress with frills around the bottom that clung to my body and looked good on me, put on make-up, and picked out jewellery to wear. I was ready early and waiting in the lounge when Stephen arrived just after 6:00. He gave me flowers and little gifts from his shop, and then he read out a poem he had written for me:

This is a copy of the poem he gave to me:-

To Suzie

Thank you for agreeing, to come on a date with me
Forgive me for being awkward, I'm as nervous as can be

My plan is to get to know you, and find out all I can
And slowly over time, perhaps I can be your man

I don't want to come on strong, or take you by surprise
Forgive me if you catch me, looking lovingly in your eyes

I'm not looking for a fling, I don't want a one-night stand
But I would really be happy, if you let me hold your hand

I think you are really nice, I really like your style
I like it when you laugh, I love it when you smile

What I've learnt of you so far, has got me interested
I'm happy to take things further, so fate can be tested

But if you find that I'm, not what you're looking for
Don't be afraid to say so, and show me to the door

I will understand, I know you don't mean to offend
Don't be scared to talk to me, I can be just a friend

If you find you like me, than please grant my wish
When the night is ending, please let me feel your kiss

Fond thoughts,
Stephen

I was flattered; he was so romantic.

Stephen then took me to a restaurant overlooking the ocean at the Entrance. We sat in front of a huge glass window, and as we talked, the huge full moon came up over the ocean, which made the atmosphere even more romantic. We ordered our food, and had a drink, even though I'm not a big drinker and Stephen said he rarely drank. We told each other all about ourselves, and Stephen was talking about creating our own reality and he told me about a comprehensive list of all the qualities he was looking for in a future partner that he had made a few years before, after breaking up with his partner, and that he had already ticked off the items that I already fulfilled on his list and that he wanted to find out if he could tick off the other items. He also said that his astrology chart at the start of that year had said he would meet that special someone around Easter, so he was hoping that it was me. I was a little surprised by this, I thought it was a bit odd to have a list, but my first thought was, *I hope I fit the list!* I barely knew Stephen but I felt an instant connection to him and I was comfortable with everything we talked about.

Stephen was very open with me as he told me more about himself. He said that he had a fifteen-year-old daughter, Amanda, and a two-and-a-half-year-old son, Eythan, both with his ex-partner. They had been together for over fourteen years and continued seeing each other off and on for a few years after they broke up, so Eythan was born eighteen months after their break-up. We then talked a lot about spiritual matters and our beliefs. He really listened when I talked, and he seemed very understanding; everything about him was just amazing. We had a great night, and I don't even remember what we ate.

After dinner, Stephen drove me home. I invited him in for a cuppa, and we talked for another half an hour before he got up to leave. We kissed passionately for a few minutes, but I told him we should get to know each other better before we went further. He was fine with that, as he was in no rush. It was the nicest date. I really liked Stephen and hoped he liked me just as much.

The next morning, Ian came down with the kids in the car he had bought for me. I was so happy when he gave me the keys. Now I had a car, and I knew I was at the start of something big.

Later that afternoon Stephen called me, and we arranged to meet the next day at 1:00 p.m. at a nearby beach that I liked. I brought my kids, and Stephen helped them dig holes in the sand and build sandcastles, and he even buried them and sculpted the sand over them, turning Jacob into a racing car and Shaylee into a mermaid. The kids took to him just like I had. At the end of the afternoon, everything they said was Stephen this and Stephen that. Stephen and I kissed again on the beach. I repeated that we should wait a while before we began anything intimate, and he confirmed that he was in no rush and would be happy to wait if I wanted him to. He had to leave at 4:30 to get ready for work that night, but we arranged to meet again the next day. We spent time together every day after this, and after five weeks, he asked me to move in with him. Everything was moving fast, but it felt right, and I was comfortable with my decision to accept his invitation. I gave a week's notice at my flat, and six weeks after our first date, we were living together.

Stephen's mother and stepfather moved out of the residence attached to the shop and went back to their home in Cessnock, leaving Stephen and I to live together. My children still came every weekend, and Stephen's son came every second weekend.

Stephen's daughter stayed with us only a couple of times in the following few months and didn't talk to me much at all.

Stephen continued working part-time as a chef, and I helped him in the shop when he was working. I loved doing this; it was relaxing, as it was never busy, but the nicest people came in to shop to browse. Sometimes when Pat and Arthur came down to visit, they watched the shop so Stephen and I could go out together, which was great.

However, my mother did not want to meet Stephen, not until we had been together for at least six months. She had seen me go through too many relationships in which I had never been happy and that didn't last. No one knew better about all that I had been through than my mum, she did meet Stephen well before six months, though, not long after I had moved in with him when Stephen took me over to her unit to pick up Blake. Mum met Stephen only very briefly, a few weeks later, when the following happened.

When I was out with Mum, we went to a shop that Mum had bought shoes from the day before, and Mum went up to the shop assistant, presented the invoice, and explained that she wanted to return a pair of shoes. The assistant responded quite aggressively, demanding to know why she wanted to return them. Mum explained that although she had tried the shoes on and they had seemed to fit when she was in the shop the day before, after she had returned home and tried the shoes on again in her unit, she noticed that they hurt her feet.

The shop assistant then called Mum a stupid old cow. I was appalled and jumped to mum's defence, telling the lady that she could not talk to my mum that way, and then the assistant got right up in my face and yelled at me. I put my hands up and pushed her out of my personal space and said, "Excuse me, there is no need to get right in my face like that," but I don't think she heard a word I said. As soon as I touched her, she yelled out for security. A nearby officer came over, and the shop assistant told him that I had pushed her and that she wanted to charge me with assault.

The security guard escorted Mum and me out of the shop and was very nice to us. He told us that as the woman had said she wanted to charge me, the police would be called. However, they most likely would want to hear my side of the story before they did anything, so I gave him my contact details. Then mum and I left (with no refund).

I wanted to call in at Little Arrows to tell Stephen that the police may be calling in to talk to me, so Mum came with me, and that's when she got to meet Stephen. Pat and Arthur were also there, and they couldn't believe that I had stood up to this woman, as I was so gentle and soft-natured. They told me that they were proud of me.

The police turned up not long after Mum and I got to the shop, and after talking to me, they let me off with a warning. Mum had about an hour to talk with Stephen, Pat, and Arthur.

After living with Stephen for a few months, things were going great. I looked after the shop while he worked at the restaurant, but when he was at the shop, I was free to spend my time doing what I liked. I had more money because I was no longer paying rent and was doing readings in the shop more often, so I was able to do some things I couldn't afford before.

One of these was a video of my singing. I had recorded a couple of my songs professionally just before I met Stephen, so I decided to use some money that I had saved to have a video clip done for "On Top of the World." This cost almost two thousand dollars, and I sent it to record companies in hopes that someone would like it enough to sign a record deal with me. I had no responses, but the copy that I had sent to the music TV show *Rage* was played on air, which was very exciting. The producers had told me which date it would be played, so we looked up the schedule, and found it listed for 3:15 a.m., Stephen and I set the alarm and got up to watch it. I never went any further with my singing career, but I still love to sing, and I do hope to one day have the money to record an album of spiritual songs.

Stephen helped me to send out copies of my songs to record companies and supported me and my goals in many other ways, including making me business cards for my mediumship work.

I joined a local gym and worked out twice each week, but my depression and anxiety continued, however, and so did my confidence issues and emotional fragility, although I still saw psychologists and counsellors each month, and was on medication. I felt scared and anxious before readings, afraid of not coping with my kids, and fearful of having another break down. Any little problem could cause intense anxiety and panic; my frequent migraine headaches continued, too, and sometimes I spent days in bed. I often worried and looked at situations negatively without realizing it. Stephen made me more aware of this and showed me more positive ways of thinking. He gave me confidence. He complimented me often, would talk me through difficult situations, and helped me keep from letting my emotions control me.

Stephen became my personal therapist who was on call 24/7, always positive, and always ready with words of encouragement and advice. I don't know where my life would be now if I hadn't met Stephen; I see him as a gift sent from God. He sees me as an angel and tells others how wonderful I am all the time.

It took me a lot of years to realize I didn't value myself or think I was good enough. Through my doubts, anxiety and negativity, Stephen was like a beacon, and he helped me change the way I looked at life and myself. I still have issues with negative feelings and thoughts at times today, but now my entire life is so positive that it is much easier to overcome them.

One lovely Saturday afternoon, Stephen closed the shop while plenty of daylight was left, and we took the kids for a walk down by the lake on the paved walkway about two kilometres long. We walked to the end, past play areas and picnic areas to a long jetty where people fished. A lot of families rode bikes and jogged along the path.

At the end of the jetty, a few people, including two young boys, were fishing. These boys were down on a lower platform doing something with one of their fishing rods, and another fishing rod lay on the upper platform where we were. As we approached, Stephen put his hand on Eythan's shoulder and said, "Be careful, Eythan. Don't step on the kids' fishing rod." Eythan was almost three by then and still small, and he kept near Stephen. We thought nothing more of this and as we continued down the jetty and then turned back.

We had only walked a few hundred metres down the path when two men ran up behind us yelling at us to stop. I didn't know what was going on, but as they reached us, I noticed that they were covered in tattoos and had muscles on their muscles; they looked like they had been working out in the prison yard. They seemed really angry, and I could smell alcohol on them as well.

They asked if we had just come from the jetty, and Stephen said yes and asked why. They responded that their boys had just come home crying and had told them that the young boy with us had stepped on one of their fishing rods and broken it!

I was scared, as the men clenched their fists and seemed ready to fight. Stephen remained calm but stood his ground, telling them that his son had not broken the fishing rod and hadn't stepped on it. The men told Stephen that he was full of crap, swore at him, and threatening to punch him out if he didn't give them the money to replace the rod.

I stepped away to a safe distance with the children while Stephen continued to talk to them. I was shaking and thought for sure that these two men would hurt Stephen. I even stopped another man who was passing, told him about the threats, and asked if he could help. He took a look at the two muscle-bound men, apologized, and suggested I call the police. I didn't know what to do, so I just stayed back and watched, praying to God and my angels for help.

Stephen continued talking for about fifteen minutes, and at one stage he got his wallet out and gave one of the men his business card. The other man then tried to grab the wallet out of Stephen's hand, but somehow Stephen managed to hold on to it and put it back in his pocket. Shortly after, the men turned and walked away, and Stephen joined me.

I asked him if he was all right, and he said he was. When I asked what had happened, and he said that he had explained things to the men and suggested they go back and ask their boys what really happened, and he emphasized that even if Eythan had stepped on the fishing rod, he was only two years old and couldn't have broken a rod lying flat on the jetty just by stepping on it. He gave them the business card so that they could come up to the shop later if they still had a problem and said that he would replace the rod with one of his own then.

I told Stephen that I thought they were going to punch him and asked him if he had been worried, and he said he had been a bit worried but that in this kind of situation it was best to stay calm and not react aggressively, as the situation would then have turned ugly. Although he had been worried for me and the children, he could handle himself but didn't want me and the kids to get hurt or see him fighting.

I was still worried. "What if they come up to the shop? You shouldn't have told them where you work," I said, but Stephen told me not to worry. He didn't think they would turn up once they had time to process what he had said, but if they did, he would handle them. Thankfully, we didn't see the men again, and I was so proud of Stephen for remaining calm through all of it. It took me some time to stop shaking and settle down, however.

In August of that year, only a couple of months after I moved in with Stephen, Blake wanted to move back in with me, as he missed me. He had talked to his dad, and Ian gave me a call, saying that if I took Blake, then I had to take Jacob and Shaylee too. Ian and Fiona were about to have a child together, so my having the older kids would take some pressure off Fiona. Ian was willing to reverse our arrangement, with my having the children during the week and his having them on weekends. The thought of this scared me.

Was I ready? How would this affect my relationship with Stephen? Would I be able to cope this time?

When I talked to Stephen about it, he reassured me that it would be fine, as he would help me and support me. I wouldn't be doing it alone this time. He seemed to really want me to take the kids, and he loved having family around him, so my children all came to live with me. They arrived during the September holidays. Blake was in year four, Jacob was in kindergarten, and Shaylee was almost four and would start preschool the following year.

Stephen had taken on a full-time head chef position at a nearby golf club to bring in more money, as the shop didn't bring in enough money to cover its costs. Stephen's wages subsidized it, which didn't leave us a lot of money to live on. Stephen had borrowed some money for the business around the time I met him, but that had gone to cover old debts and restocking. We managed with what we had, which wasn't a lot.

When we took the kids on, I stopped going to the gym, as I couldn't find the time between watching the shop for Stephen and having the kids hanging off me and demanding attention. Stephen did cook all the meals at home, however, and he often spoiled me with some really beautiful food, and I also found myself binge eating chocolate whenever I felt stressed or anxious, which was quite often. Combined with the lack of exercise, this caused me to put on a little weight. Not a lot at first, but the weight gain continued over the years.

Stephen also took over the meditation classes when Joan moved away, and everyone enjoyed his meditations. He wrote his own meditations, and his deep, soothing voice was very relaxing as he talked group members through the sessions. He also gave out hand-outs each week to help people make improvements in their lives, and he made scones and cakes for the group. The meditation still lasted about thirty minutes, but everyone stayed for at least an hour and a half talking, and everyone who came all became good friends.

Stephen was great with the children, and they loved him and talked about him all the time when they were with their dad. Eythan got on really well with my kids as well. With their blond hair and blue eyes, and being about the same height, Shaylee and Eythan looked almost like twins, and when my kids were together with Stephen's, an outsider couldn't tell that they were from different families.

Stephen earned the children's respect, but he could be hard on them at times and raised his voice if they did something wrong or were being naughty. He never hit them, but both the children and I were afraid that he might when he seemed really angry. I would worry that the kids may feel I let them down by not protecting them from this angry man, so I stuck up for them and tried to keep them away from him when he was like this.

This was the only real issue in our relationship, and we talked about the subject many times. Stephen maintained that we had to discipline the children or they would walk all over us and have no self-control, but I found disciplining the children hard to do. He got upset with me for not using any discipline, and I got upset with him for being too strict, and I noticed that he could be harder on my children than on Eythan. I brought the issue of favouritism up with him, and he admitted to it but said he couldn't help it, and he also pointed out that I, too, treated my children differently than Eythan. He did his best to fill the role of a Stepfather and was active in raising my children, treating them like his own as much as possible. On my part, I did love Eythan but I didn't try to take the place of his mother and wasn't as active in raising him as I was with my own children.

One time, when I was lying down with Shaylee, Stephen was in the kitchen cooking dinner while Jacob and Blake were in the lounge, and Jacob and Blake started a fight. Stephen came out and asked what was going on, to which Blake replied that Jacob spat on him. Stephen told Blake to tell him if Jacob did this again instead of taking matters into his own hands, and he explained to Jacob, "Spit comes from inside your body and is full of germs, so spitting on your brother is no different than throwing poo at him." He ended by saying that if Jacob did this again, he would stick his finger up his bum and wipe poo on Jacob's face to see how he liked it.

Stephen then went back into the kitchen, and a few minutes later, Blake yelled out that Jacob was spitting on him again. Stephen heard this, stuck his finger into a jar of Nutella chocolate spread, and came back into the lounge pretending to have his hand down the back of his pants. He then extended his hand towards the boys so they could see the brown stuff on it. Stephen then reached forward and wiped his finger on Jacob's face. Both Blake screamed, and Jacob screamed louder. He was mortified! Then Stephen stood back and licked the rest of the Nutella off his finger. Blake had seen him do this and was almost sick; Jacob was still too busy screaming to notice. Stephen looked at Blake and said, "What's the matter? It's only Nutella. You didn't think I would really stick my finger up my bum did you?"

Jacob was still screaming, so he hadn't heard anything that was said, and when I came out to see what was going on, I found him with tears running down his face and became really upset.

Stephen told me what had happened, I comforted Jacob, and once he realized that Stephen had tricked him, he settled down. Stephen had traumatized Jacob, so I thought Stephen had gone too far, and we had a fight about this. I still don't like that Stephen did this, and I cringed when writing about it.

Looking back now, I can see there is a funny side to the story, but this wasn't the only time he traumatized us by doing silly things like this. Stephen calls it "shock treatment" and says that a parent has to back up his or her threats so the kids know that they can't get away with bad behaviour. However, I am thankful that Stephen didn't smack the kids or otherwise physically discipline them. Jacob never did spit on Blake again, and now that the kids are older, they don't have the same issues with their behaviour.

When Jacob was younger, he often got in trouble at school and was suspended many times, also when the kids had problems, Jacob was usually involved. We took Jacob to counsellors and on their suggestion, enrolled him in courses designed to help children with expressing feelings in a healthy way and manage anger. Stephen and I also took a parenting course to help us cope with this behaviour. This all helped, but the problems continued, and when we finally exhausted all solutions a few years later when Jacob was eight, he was diagnosed with ADHD and put on medication. Jacob took the medication only when he went to school, and it made a huge difference in his behaviour at school straight away. By the end of primary school, he was elected as a school leader, and he was the best bell ringer the school ever had. By the time he started high school, he no longer needed the medication and stopped taking it.

Stephen has been a good communicator as long as I've known him. I found that he kept no secrets and told no lies, and he would talk about anything, to the point that he gave too much information, and, as I've joked, he suffered from foot-in-mouth disease. He could analyse a situation from many angels and describe each perspective in detail. Sometimes when he explained things to me, I thought, *Surely he knows that I'm not so dumb that I don't understand that already*, but a lot of the time he did help me to understand the idea better or to look at something in a new way.

Stephen helped me work through many issues. When I would get upset and go into the bed room to cry, I would call him in after a while and ask him if he realized that I had been upset and was crying, and he would say that he knew but that this was my issue and not his and that I needed to work through it on my own first. I asked if we could talk now, and he came to talk to me to help me through what was bothering me. I always felt better after we talked, and over time I found that I didn't need to see counsellors as much because I was starting to cope better.

Another thing Stephen liked to do was to write down his goals for the coming year, as he was a big believer in making his intentions clear, and he talked about this many times. He went to a seminar in Newcastle a few years before we met about the power of the mind, and the concepts made some sense to me when he explained them, but what convinced me to adopt this way of thinking was the DVD *The Secret*, about the Law of Attraction. Stephen and I watched it together, and I was so impressed by this film and felt a real connection to its message, so I started writing down my goals and making vision boards, as the film suggests.

Over the years I have been amazed at how well these practices have attracted what I want to my life. I didn't always notice much change straight away, as changing old habits and thought patterns took a while, but when I look back, I realize how many goals I've achieved and material things I've attracted, and am truly amazed. I am now a big believer in the Law of Attraction, and I often suggest that others learn about it and practice its principles.

Stephen would do almost anything for anyone, even someone he barely knew, and this has included offering our shed to people going through hard times who needed somewhere to stay. He didn't check with me first, as he was afraid I would focus on the negative possibilities and would worry.

In one instance, a lovely young woman named Courtney, who had come to the shop to have a reading with me, and had visited the shop a couple of times after this. Courtney was talking to Stephen and told him that she had an abusive boyfriend and needed somewhere to stay for a few weeks until she found a place of her own. Stephen invited her to stay in the shed, set up a bedroom for her, and helped her move her things in. Courtney and I became friends, almost like sisters, as we had a lot in common, and talked and laughed often. However, I was a little uncomfortable with her staying with us, as she was very good-looking, and Stephen and I had only been together for a few months and living together for only about eight weeks. Courtney realized that I was uncomfortable and a little jealous, and she didn't want to cause any trouble, so she didn't stay more than a few weeks. Unfortunately, she didn't keep in contact after she left.

The next person to reside in our shed was a man who had fallen out with his flatmate and encountered financial trouble. He stayed with us until he got the money together to move into a one-bedroom apartment a few months later. He was a nice man and mostly kept to himself, coming into our house only to use the amenities. He cooked on a portable gas stove, and the shed was equipped with a small fridge, TV, and lounge. I was uncomfortable having him there, too, but any problems we had with him were in my head.

Stephen offered help whenever he could in other ways, too, even if he had to go out of his way to do so, and he never asked for anything in return, but he also didn't approve these other methods of help with me, either. This could be frustrating, as these situations often affected the whole family. I sometimes felt he was too generous and allowed people to take advantage of him, but he didn't seem to mind. He's helped so many lovely people over the years that I am much more used to it now.

Stephen also has a quick wit and great sense of humour, although at times it can be a bit twisted, or rude, crude, and socially undesirable, as he calls it. One time when I was sitting in the office at the back of Little Arrows with Stephen, eating my lunch, when Luey, a regular visitor to the shop and its neighbours, came in. He was a retired older man originally from Malta, and although he had moved to Australia in his early twenties, he still had a strong accent. On this particular day, he noticed a new water fountain in the shop and complimented Stephen on its looks, and then he put his hand in the water, took a little sip, and said that the water even tasted beautiful. He asked what Stephen had put into it to make it taste so good, and Stephen responded quite casually, "Oh, I pissed in it." Luey spat out the water and wiped his mouth. I sprayed food out of my mouth and burst out laughing. I couldn't believe Stephen had just said that! I still giggle every time I tell this story. The look on Luey's face was priceless.

After the kids moved in with us full-time, I had a lot of trouble coping with the kids at night while Stephen was at work, and I often called him to tell him about the little dramas that seemed so big in the moment, particularly Jacob's fights with Blake that escalated out of control. Stephen tried to talk me or the kids through the situation. Then, not long afterwards, Stephen cut back his hours to a casual position at the restaurant so that he could give me more support.

And he did support me and encourage me in everything I did or wanted to do. He did so much around the house. In addition to the cooking, he did the dishes and helped with the laundry and general housekeeping. He was also very romantic, saying the most beautiful things to me and doing romantic things, too. He wrote me dozens of poems, including this one from early in our relationship:

My Sweet Suzie

We got off on a good start, we seem to be compatible
I found the things I thought of you are more than tangible

I am so happy to have met you, now I feel sure
You are the one I wanted to find, who I've been looking for

You fill my days with sunshine, and my heart with love
You touch my soul in special ways, like an angel from above

My body now burns for you, with a strong desire
Every thought I have of you, seems to feed the fire

I feel proud to be with you, I am a lucky man
To have someone so wonderful, to take me by the hand

I want to give you all I can, to fill your life with bliss
I want to show tenderness and caress you with my kiss

I will do all within my power, to keep you safe from strife
For I feel that together, we will have a happy life

I will never do you wrong, or betray your trust
I will always listen to you and do the things I must

I give to you my heart, with all my love inside
I keep from you no secrets, there is nothing left to hide

So, Suzie, when you read this, know that this is true
You make me happy as can be, I'm so in love with you

On 23 November 2005, Stephen received a call from his ex-sister-in-law to let him know that his ex-wife, Jannelle, had passed away. Jannelle had been diagnosed with a terminal brain tumour five years earlier, before she and Stephen had broken up. The tumour had placed a great deal of emotional and financial pressure on their relationship. Stephen had issues with Jannelle's family as well, and they both found it hard to cope. This all affected their relationship and contributed to their break-up.

I only met Jannelle once, not long after I moved in with Stephen, when we travelled to Cessnock to pick up Eythan. Stephen took me inside to meet Jannelle, and we had a cup of coffee and sat out the back and talked for a little while. I found her to be very friendly.

About two months later, we found out that Jannelle's tumour had grown back. Doctors had tried operating on her again, but there wasn't much more that they could do, so the time she had left was limited. Therefore, it wasn't a big surprise when Jannelle's sister called with the news of her passing, but Stephen was very sad just the same.

Then, on a Saturday afternoon in early December, the kids were at their dad's and I went to the beach and then out shopping before I went back to the shop around 3:30. Stephen was sitting at the computer in the office, where he could see into the shop in case someone came in. When I walked in, suddenly my guides said that Stephen had gotten me a Christmas present, and I felt that it was nearby.

I asked Stephen whether this were true, and he said no, but I could tell straight away that he was lying, so I said, "Yes you do." He tried to tell me that he had been in the shop all day and hadn't gone anywhere to get anything when an image of a ring flashed through my mind. "It's a ring," I said. He continued to deny it, but I wasn't having any of that and told him that I wanted to see it.

Reluctantly, he went over to a cupboard, reached in, and pulled out a ring set to show me. He explained that our friend Natalie, who was also a psychic and did readings in the shop, had been visited by her late grandmother, who told her to give Stephen this ring, a family heirloom. Natalie brought it over earlier that day, and Stephen was thrilled, as he had told her that he had wanted to get an engagement ring but had been having financial problems. However, even though he couldn't afford a new ring, he could afford to have this ring resized and polished. He couldn't believe it and was so grateful to Natalie and her late gran.

He then said that it was unfair that he hadn't been able to keep it a secret from me and was disappointed that I had made him show me, as he had intended to have it sized and then surprise me with a proper proposal on Christmas Day. I told him I was sorry I had spoiled his surprise but that it was my guides' fault. I told him to give the ring to me at Christmas as he had planned and that I would say yes when he did. This made him happy, and we talked at length about when to get married, where, and other plans. We set a date for the following spring, 24 September 2006, and decided to keep the guest list to just a few friends and some family members and to get married in the backyard of Stephen's mum's house in Cessnock.

When Christmas came, I got engaged to my husband, Stephen Price, and he wrapped the ring with the following poem:

Proposal

Suzie, I have a feeling, you are the girl for me
In the time we've been together, you have made me so happy

I love you in so many ways, each day I love you more
And as I search my heart and mind it only makes me sure

I know you are not everything yet, that you strive to be
But just to watch you trying makes it easy for me to see

The effort that you put in with all your heart and soul
Has shown me to the light and helped to make me whole

Your children are a blessing, each and every one
They make our life more interesting, as well as much more fun

I appreciate the love you give and the affection that you show
Knowing each other completely has helped our love to grow

Together we both learn and grow in many varied ways
I want this to continue, until the end of our days

I have learnt to trust my feelings and the vibes I get
So I ask this question easily without one regret

I would go down on one knee and shout out for all to hear
I love you, Suzie Daubert, and I always want you near

I'd be honoured if you would agree to stay with me for life
Please say that you will marry me and agree to be my wife

Your Loving Partner,
Stephen

The next nine months went quickly. The kids had settled into school well and made friends, and Stephen and I became closer and closer. He had started proceedings in the family court system to get custody of Eythan, who was living with Jannelle's parents, as he had his entire life. I think Amanda, who was now sixteen and a half, was angry at Stephen for trying to get custody of Eythan, as Jannelle had wanted her parents to raise him, and Amanda avoided him when he went to pick up Eythan. I don't know what issues Amanda had with Stephen, but she definitely had issues with him. Stephen tried not to let this non-relationship affect him, but it did, as I saw him crying about her often. Even today, although they do speak to each other, Amanda doesn't have much to do with him and has never taken time to get to know him or me. Yet Stephen is hopeful that one day he can be in her life more and will be open to that when she's ready. The legal process was long and drawn out and expensive.

Before our wedding, Stephen was given two tickets from his book supplier connected to the publisher Hay House to see the American author Doreen Virtue in Sydney. Stephen asked his mum to watch the shop and the kids for the day, and he and I headed down to Sydney for the show. We were both very excited, especially when we found our seats just a couple of rows from the front. I told Stephen several times on the way down that I would get a reading from Doreen, but he was sceptical that I'd be able to, and he was even more sceptical after we arrived to find more than two thousand people in the audience. He told me not to get my hopes up, but I told him that I was sure that she would pick me and asked him what I should ask when she did. He didn't offer much advice, but I was ready anyway.

The first half of the show came and went. Doreen was great, and everyone in the audience was in awe at her amazing presence and great speaking ability. The readings she did were really good. Then, during the second half of the show, she introduced her husband, who talked for some time about animal guides, and then Doreen came back on. Towards the end of her show, she said that she would do one more reading, and people everywhere, including me, put their hands up. Doreen looked around and then looked straight at me and pointed. "You," she said. "The lady near the front, with the big smile."

I said very excitedly, "Me?"

She said yes and told one of her helpers to give me a microphone.

Doreen asked me if I had a question, and I did. I told her that I was a psychic medium and also a singer-songwriter, and I asked her which path should I concentrate on pursuing. She asked me to sing a few lines from one of my songs, so I sang a few verses acapella. I then stopped for a minute, and the audience gave me a huge round of applause.

Doreen said simply, "Well, I think there is your answer!" She said I had a beautiful voice and thanked me for sharing my singing. After the show, quite a few people came up to me to compliment my singing. I felt special and proud, and Stephen was also very proud of me.

As I pursued my singing, I kept hitting roadblocks and nothing had happened, but over time, more and more people wanted to book psychic readings with me, so this road was smooth and steady. I've noticed that when things continually block your progress in a certain direction, it generally happens for a reason, but if things instead go smoothly, then you're heading in the direction you're meant to travel. At that point, my singing career just sort of dropped away, and I focused more on doing readings.

I still experienced anxiety before readings, and I told Stephen I didn't like doing more than a couple of readings each day, as I would feel quite drained after each one.

My energy level was particularly low at this point in my life because of the energy I spent worrying and feeling anxious and depressed. Stephen had to get the kids up and ready for school, as I needed twelve to fourteen hours of sleep a night. I regularly went to bed at 8:00 or 8:30 p.m. and got up around 10:00 or 11:00 a.m. If I didn't sleep this long, then I had no energy during the day and would need an afternoon nap just to get through.

Late one Saturday night when my kids were at their dad's and Stephen had Eythan for the weekend, I went to bed but Eythan wanted to stay up to watch a video, so Stephen stayed up with him. They lay on the lounge with a two-bar electric heater on in front of them on the floor to keep them warm.

Then, something woke me up. The clock read a little after 2:00 a.m. Stephen hadn't come to bed yet, so I figured he must have fallen asleep on the lounge, but I didn't feel like getting up to find out, so I didn't, thinking he would come in later if he woke up. A few minutes later, I heard a bit of a commotion coming from the lounge room and Eythan crying. I wondered what was happening but figured Stephen would come in soon, so I waited. Stephen came in a few minutes later with Eythan, who was still crying. I could tell something was wrong straight away, as Stephen called out to me as he came in. I sat up and asked him what was wrong. "We had a fire!" he said.

I asked if they were all right, and Stephen said, "Eythan is, but I'm not. I burnt my leg." He then explained that he had fallen asleep on the lounge with Eythan, and a few minutes before, something had woken him from a deep sleep. When he opened his eyes, he saw that a pillow had fallen on top of the heater, and before he could grab it, it burst into flames. He quickly jumped up to extinguish the pillow, but had forgotten Eythan was lying with him, and Eythan fell on the floor and woke suddenly.

Eythan started crying, as he was scared and didn't know what was happening. Stephen grabbed him, ran him into the kids' room, and set him on the bed with instructions to stay there. Then he ran back into the lounge room.

Stephen tried to pull the pillow off the heater, but only half of it came away, as it had melted through the middle. He dropped the half pillow on the floor, knelt in front of the heater, and smothered the fire with a blanket, but he realized that the heater was still plugged in and turned on. He jumped over to unplug it, but he accidently knelt on the smouldering half pillow, which stuck to and burnt his knee. He managed to put the fire out after that, and after he put the heater and burnt pillow outside, he got Eythan and then came to me. The whole thing had taken only a couple of minutes. His knee still had melted pillow stuck to it and looked black. He said he didn't need to go to the hospital, as the burn would be fine if treated with ice and then fresh aloe vera.

Stephen didn't get much sleep after that, as he was in considerable pain. The next day he put some ointment and a bandage on the burn, and on Monday, when he went to chemist to get some new bandages and ointment, the chemist suggested that Stephen go to the doctor's, as the burn looked bad. Stephen reluctantly did so.

At the office, the doctor peeled off part of the melted pillow that was still stuck to Stephen's knee and said that Stephen had a third-degree burn, dressed it, and suggested that he may need plastic surgery, but Stephen refused that treatment. The doctor then arranged for a nurse to come to our place to change the dressing each day for about a week, and the burn healed quickly, but Stephen was left with a big scar on his knee. We also had to fix a big hole in the carpet.

I really feel that my late nan had woken me from my sleep that night and then woken Stephen when I didn't get out of bed. I am sure that if she hadn't done this, the fire would have been much worse. I am so blessed that I have such a strong connection with my guides and spirit family, who always watch over me and my family, it's little things like the protection and guidance they provide that I really appreciate.

As I gained more experience doing readings, I found it hard to connect with certain people and bring through messages for them. I did have palm reading to fall back on during these sessions, but to ensure clients were happy with their spiritual readings, I decided to learn other techniques as backup. I had long had an interest in tarot cards and found out that a lady in a nearby suburb taught tarot card courses, so during the nine months between the engagement and wedding, I enrolled in one of the courses, and when I completed it, I enrolled in and completed the advanced course. I memorized the meanings of all the cards, and after a few months, when I was comfortable using them, I incorporated them into my readings. I started each reading using my mediumship, and now I also did a card spread, and if there was enough time, I would then read the client's palm. This new addition boosted my confidence in my readings, and because the cards could be quite accurate, clients liked them.

Around this time, I had a few problems with Ian's wife, Fiona, a devout Christian. She went to church every Sunday and had a strong belief that all psychics were evil and worked with the devil. I had met people with this belief before and didn't pay any attention to them, but my children spent each weekend with her, and she shared her views about my work with them. The idea that I would burn in hell scared Jacob and Shaylee (Blake was old enough to not listen), and they were often emotional when they returned home and told me to stop doing psychic readings. I explained that I worked with God and angels, so what I did wasn't evil and they didn't need to be scared for me and shouldn't listen to Fiona.

When I spoke with Ian about this, he, too, was angry with Fiona and said that he would talk to her. Fiona's beliefs were set, however, and she didn't agree with Ian on this subject and continued to get into my children's heads. This caused further problems in the months that followed.

I received a personal letter from Fiona that was very judgemental and quite offensive. She put me down for doing psychic readings and said again that I would burn in hell and was evil. She quoted the Bible to back up her claims, and her tone was aggressive and rude. Stephen helped me to write a response that explained my belief that what I was doing was natural and that I worked with God. We also quoted the Bible, showing passages that contradicted her claims. Some of these sentences even came from the same paragraphs as her quotes. We pointed out that the Bible is full of contradictions and emphasized that I worked with loving and positive spirits, not the devil.

Unfortunately, she didn't take any of this on board. This remained an issue for some time between us, and it also caused problems between her and Ian, as Ian also didn't like her forcing her views on the children. Fortunately, my children believed what I told them and eventually learnt not to listen to her claims.

By this time, Stephen's shop really wasn't working out, as it was losing about thirty thousand dollars a year. Stephen was also paying maintenance for his children, which wasn't a lot but did make things more difficult. The extra money from Stephen's chef job didn't cover the shortfall, so Stephen needed to borrow more money to catch up on his debts to suppliers and his lawyer, not to mention to pay for the wedding and honeymoon. Stephen talked to his mother about using her home again as collateral for the loan, explaining his plan to pay off his business debts, close the shop just before our wedding, and then get a full-time job to pay off the rest of the new loan. He had been in the shop for over two and a half years, and his three-year lease on the premises was almost up.

Pat agreed, so she and Stephen arranged a loan from the bank: Stephen borrowed another fifty thousand dollars, which now gave him one hundred thousand dollars in loans to repay. He paid for lawyers' fees, put some money aside for our wedding and honeymoon, used most of the rest to pay off the outstanding debts, and then gave his mother five thousand dollars to thank her for all her support. He closed the business about a week before our wedding.

My mother was worried about my getting married again because I had made some bad choices with men in the past and she didn't want me to rush into marriage with Stephen. I totally understood her view and knew she only wanted me to be happy, but I was in love, and I had never felt this strongly about any man before. Mum chose not to come to the wedding, as it was far for her to travel, and she wouldn't know anyone there. This decision hurt me, but I didn't mention my feelings, as I had to accept her choice. No matter what, I'll always love her, and although we may not always see things the same way, I know she acts out of deep love for me.

Stephen and I travelled to Cessnock on Saturday, 23 September, the day before the wedding. We stayed the night in a cabin at a caravan park. Stephen's nephew Jerome was having his twenty-first birthday and engagement party at Stephen's mum's home the night before our wedding, so we went to the party to relax. A lot of Stephen's relatives attended, so I got to meet many of them, and we had a lovely night, although we did leave around 10:00.

The next morning, Stephen took the boys to his mum's to get ready, and Shaylee and I went to get our hair and make-up done. We arrived at Pat's place and the boys were waiting out the front, and then the ceremony began.

Shaylee was the flower girl, Eythan was the ring bearer, Jacob was page boy, and Blake walked me down the aisle to meet Stephen, who stood with his best man, Adam, and the celebrant. Then, before a few of my friends, a few of Stephen's friends, and many members of Stephen's big family, we exchanged the vows we had written. It was a beautiful sunny day but was not too hot, as a light breeze and some large gusts of wind blew. We had lots of photos taken in the gardens with Stephen and me and all the guests, and then we had the reception in the back courtyard.

Stephen's mum had done all of the catering, as she had for Jerome's party the night before, as she was a retired chef and cake decorator. We had simple finger foods, but Pat had done a lot of work to get everything ready. Pat also made and beautifully decorated our wedding cake. We had a wonderful wedding day and were very happy.

That night, we travelled back to our home in Long Jetty, but a couple of days later, after taking my kids to their dad's, Stephen and I caught a plane to the Whitsunday Islands off the coast of Queensland, a bus, and then a ferry to a resort on Long Island. We stayed there for five nights and had a great time. We went on a helicopter flight around the islands and headed out to tour the Great Barrier Reef and to go snorkelling with the fish. On the two-hour trip out to the reef, we experienced three-metre swells, making the trip quite rough, and I got seasick both going out and coming back. This is the only bad memory I have of our honeymoon, and the snorkelling was well worth it. For the rest of the trip, we lazed and had picnic lunches on the secluded beaches, went canoeing and jet skiing, and had massages, and really pampered ourselves. The food was great, too, and the swimming pool at our resort had a swim-up bar so we could enjoy cocktails while in the pool. Altogether, we had a beautiful honeymoon, and I didn't want to leave.

After we got back, Stephen and I moved out of the residence at the shop and into a house at Bateau Bay. By this time, Stephen was more than one hundred twenty thousand dollars in debt between the loan and his credit cards. I was still on a disability pension, and as I still suffered from depression and anxiety, I asked Stephen to go on to a carer's payment so that he could be with me and the children and not have to work full-time. Stephen was happy to do this for me, and he supplemented this with casual chef work.

I put my name in to do readings at a spiritualist shop in Tuggerah, and after a trial, the manager offered to have me do readings one day a week. I was only allowed thirty minutes for each reading and often went over, which the shop manager did not like, but over time, I was better able to manage the amount of time that I gave each client. I did three to five readings each day I worked, the shop charged forty five dollars each reading and took eighteen dollars from this, and I earned the remaining twenty-seven dollars per reading. Not long after I began, the manager asked me to add another day of readings, as clients had given me great feedback and many of them wanted to book future readings. I agreed.

I still suffered from migraines at this time, and sometimes I just felt unwell, and sometimes this coincided with my days to work at the shop, so Stephen would call in for me. I also started to see clients come to our home for readings and even read for groups at clients' homes.

I was now meditating every day, which helped me to be more grounded, and my readings improved. By doing so many readings at the shop, I become more confident in myself, and more spirit guides came to me to give me information during the readings. I learnt more all the time, reading many more books on spiritual topics; completing more courses, including three in reiki to become a reiki master; and participating in many spiritual groups. Despite my growth spiritually and psychically, I still suffered badly mentally and physically from anxiety and depression.

After we had lived in Bateau Bay for twelve months, Stephen's court case for custody of Eythan came to a conclusion. Stephen had run out of money to pay for his lawyer, so he had to drop the lawyer and find legal aid just weeks before the conclusion of the case. The lawyer's last bill charged over twelve thousand dollars, and Stephen had to make an arrangement to pay it off in small increments over many years. Stephen considered filing for bankruptcy, but luckily, he never did. However, he did see a financial adviser and worked out payment plans for all of his creditors. By then, he owed over one hundred and thirty thousand dollars in debts and is still paying them off slowly.

The court ruled against Stephen and awarded custody to Eythan's grandparents. Faced with seeing his son only every second weekend, he protested and asked whether he could see his son more often if he moved back to Cessnock. I was really unsure about making this move but felt I had to support Stephen, as I knew how much his son meant to him. The court then ruled that if Stephen moved back to Cessnock and remained in that area, he would be allowed to have his son Eythan five nights per fortnight instead of two and half of all holidays.

My mum was very upset when she learnt that we needed to move. While we lived on the Central Coast, Mum had been able to see the kids often and could be there for me when I needed her, too. She said she would miss having me and the children around. I was also upset and was torn between going with Stephen to Cessnock and staying on the Central Coast. Blake also didn't want to move, as he was about to start high school and didn't want to leave his friends. He preferred to move back in with his father in the Blue Mountains, where he already had friends. Ian was happy to have Blake with him if I was okay with the choice.

I talked to Stephen about all these concerns, but he already had his mind fixed on going back to Cessnock. This choice was not about my relationship with him but about his relationship with his son, who was now five and about to start kindergarten. He really felt that he needed to be there for his son, and he also wanted to repair his relationship with Amanda, who he had not spoken to since before Jannelle passed.

He loved me too, so he begged me to please come with him, promising to do everything he could to make me happy. It was such a big move, and to a place where I knew no one, so I was really scared. This choice also meant that Blake would live with Ian again, and I hated the thought of not seeing Blake as often, but I just couldn't refuse Stephen. I loved him and wanted to stay with him.

Chapter 4

Building My Business

Stephen and I moved out of the house in Bateau Bay just after Christmas 2007 but we had trouble in finding a suitable place to rent in Cessnock, so we and our kids had to move into Stephen's parents' house. Pat and Arthur were away in Queensland for two weeks when we moved and had suggested to Stephen that we could stay while they were gone, but we ended up staying for about six weeks. The house was a bit cramped, and I wasn't really comfortable, so I thought I had made a big mistake.

During those six weeks, Stephen and I applied for more than fourteen houses before we were accepted at a brand-new, modern brick home with a fully fenced yard for our puppy dogs on a new estate. The house had three bedrooms, a large lounge room, a huge dining area, kitchen, and double garage. I loved it, and it was great to have our own space again when we moved in.

Most weekends, Jacob and Shaylee went to their dad's and Blake came up to stay with us in Cessnock, and Ian and I shared the kids over the holidays. After a while, Ian's work commitments changed and he and Fiona were having trouble in their relationship, so we swapped the kids only every second or third weekend. I would try to visit my mum and stepdad, Gary, when I could, but that wasn't very often, and I could bring the kids with me even less often. Mum and I chatted on the phone most weeks, and mum and Gary stayed over in Cessnock a few times.

Stephen did casual chef work as soon as we moved, and the kids settled in at school, but I continued doing psychic readings two days a week in Tuggerah, an hour's drive from Cessnock. Stephen made some flyers to promote me as a psychic medium so I could get some local work, and we distributed these to all the hairdressing salons in town, as Stephen thought that if we could get the hairdressers talking about me, they'd generate some business with their clients. This worked really well, as I got some bookings straight away, and within two months of moving into our new house, word of mouth was spreading, and I was doing more readings at my home than at the shop in Tuggerah. I then decided to quit doing readings at the shop not just to save on the travelling but also because I no longer had to give the shop a cut of my takings.

By the time we had been in Cessnock for six months, I did readings five days a week and was booked out two weeks in advance, so Stephen suggested that I register as a business and report my earnings. This was a big step for me; I had relied on my pension for a few years, and even then it hadn't been easy to get by. I had never really thought of doing readings as a full-time business until now. It made sense, though, so Stephen and I got everything organized, and I came up with the name Ghost Whisperer Suzie for my business, registered it, and told centre link, I had officially become the provider for my family.

Although my readings were booked out so far in advance, I was still limited in how many readings I could do in a day. My readings still lasted for at least an hour, and they often went for more than an hour. I really focused in order to pick up as much information for my clients as I could, and I used a lot of energy to do this. However, because of my depression and anxiety, my energy levels were still low, so just a few readings totally wiped me out. Four readings was the most I could do, and I usually did fewer.

Stephen really helped me, and over time, my energy levels slowly improved. I still liked my sleep-ins, but I was able to stay up later in the evening, and I only needed about ten hours' sleep at most each night, depending on what I have been doing that day.

Registering my business meant that Stephen lost his carer's payment and that my pension was drastically reduced, based on our combined earnings. Stephen continued doing some casual chef work, but all of his earnings went to paying his debts, so I was left to pay for all of our living expenses, and I still wasn't charging a lot for my readings, so money was still very tight. We would be able to save a little, but then a big expense or a holiday with the kids came up and the savings would be gone.

I contacted a local Internet engineering business to have my website made, and Stephen provided them with all the information they needed and learnt how to edit the site himself. Soon after, I became a professional member of the Australian Psychic Association, which I had heard about on the television show *The One*. Some of the psychics on this show were members of the APA, so I looked the organization up on the Internet and requested the forms I needed to apply. In addition to these, the APA required that I send three affidavits from clients to affirm my psychic abilities.

Stephen had become much more than just my husband, as he took on roles as child carer, cleaner, secretary, manager, promoter, and partner in my business in many ways. Stephen took care of most of the housework and always made sure the house was clean when I had appointments booked, and he often took the kids out to the park or to visit family or friends while I did readings. He answered my emails and phone calls and took reservations for appointments. My business just continued to grow as my reputation as an accurate medium spread further, and people from Sydney, the Central Coast, and the entire Hunter area booked appointments.

In addition to my reading on spiritual topics, I took courses, including one on ThetaHealing, and I listened to motivational CDs to continue learning and improving myself.

Stephen also took on part-time work for Norm, his former boss from his head chef position, helping to teach pasta-making classes. During one class, a group of eight people asked Norm to organize a psychic to do readings during the dinner portion of a class, so Norm asked Stephen to ask me if I could do this. I decided I could.

Stephen spent the first hour of the class showing everyone how to make pasta and sauce from scratch and helping the class members as they made their own. Then, the class sat down to eat. I did short readings for each person in another room during the dinner. I had been invited to join the class at the start, but I preferred not to be in the room with everyone in case they talked about themselves, as I didn't want to know anything about people before I did their readings. If I had never met the client before a reading, he or she couldn't rationalize that I knew the things I brought out in a reading because I had overheard it. Everyone enjoyed their readings and the food, and after I worked for two hours, I had a beautiful meal ready for me.

Near the end of 2008, I saw an advertisement for a medium stage show not far from Cessnock hosted by a medium named Luke, who I had met a few times a couple of years before, we had done readings for each other, so I decided to go to watch him in action. I was impressed with the show, and afterwards, I talked with Luke for a while. He suggested that I do shows, as he thought I would be good at them, and asked if I would be interested in joining him doing a show. I was unsure, as I was scared that I wouldn't pick up any messages and that the audience wouldn't like me. When I got home, I told Stephen about Luke's suggestion, and he was full of support and encouragement, so I decided to give it a try.

Stephen and I decided it would be a good idea to do a trial first, so I went to see some friends from the Dolphin Healing Centre, a spiritual centre in Cessnock, and asked to use the centre's big room for a trial show. They were happy to help, and they even took care of inviting people and selling tickets. I also sought advice in an email to another medium who had a good reputation as a medium and had done a lot of shows around the Central Coast. His wife replied that psychic stage shows weren't easy to do, as they weren't like doing platform work at a spiritualist church, where everyone believed, making it easier to connect with the audience than in the real world, where everyone was a critic." I had not done any platform work at spiritualist churches and was a bit shocked that she had offered no positive advice and had only advised me against the show. I felt a bit disappointed and surprised that someone spiritual would be so negative and unhelpful, so I chose to disregard this advice. I got some positive advice from Luke instead.

On the night of my first show, I felt so sick on the five-minute drive to the Dolphin Healing Centre, as I was petrified, and I told Stephen that I had changed my mind and didn't want to do the show. I didn't care how many people would attend; I just wanted to call the whole thing off. Stephen wouldn't let me! He said I had made a commitment and had to go through with it, and no amount of my crying would change that. When we arrived, Stephen persuaded me to get out of the car and go inside.

I was surprised at how many people were there. The room looked full, so over forty people were sitting and waiting. I did a quick meditation to calm my nerves, and after a few minutes, Stephen went out and introduced me. When I went onstage, I spoke a little about myself. I glanced at Stephen, who was sitting over to the side, and he looked like he was praying, and he later confirmed that he was. I hoped his prayers would help. The first reading went well, as I picked up quite a few things for an audience member. No one connected with the next message, although I was sure it was meant for someone there, so I moved on. The next reading had the audience in tears. The lady I connected with had just lost her daughter and granddaughter in a car accident a few days before. I was able to describe them both in detail and also to describe some of the details of the accident and when it happened. The lady was so overcome with emotion that she couldn't speak, but her friends confirmed everything that I said.

After this reading, the rest of the performance just flowed. I did about twelve readings over two hours, and after the show, audience members took my business cards and told me what a brilliant show it was and that I was amazing. One of the ladies who came up to me said that the message no one had connected to had been meant for her, but she was too shy to have a reading done in public, so she hadn't put her hand up. She said I had perfectly described the looks and personality of the person I had named, and I had also accurately described how she died. This lady made an appointment to see me a few weeks later. I was on such a high after the show; I felt so proud of myself, as everyone had had a great night, and as we had charged ten dollars each, I had made just over four hundred dollars in just a couple of hours.

Stephen said that he was so proud of me and so impressed with how I had performed. He knew I could do it but had been worried and didn't want me to know it. Although he had heard great things about my readings from clients, this was the first time he had seen me in action, and he said the specific details I gave in the readings had impressed him the most, as psychics and mediums often only gave general information. In my readings, I started out with general information and then gave more detail as I went, and Stephen said that this validated the message. He told me that he saw people's jaws drop and looks of shock on their faces as I did readings.

This was the first of many shows in many towns and cities on the East Coast of Australia both by myself and with other mediums. Turnout has varied, with only a few people attending on some nights, and I've even called shows off on the night because only one or two people showed up, but then there have been shows with large audiences. As my reputation grew, I attracted bigger and bigger numbers to my shows.

I got busier and busier in my private readings after the first show, too, and I was booked out farther and farther in advance. In addition to this and shows every month or two, I travelled to do psychic parties in people's houses in other towns. Often I stayed in another town for a few days, and Stephen came with me to take care of me if the kids were at their father's; otherwise, Stephen stayed home with the kids and I travelled alone and looked after myself.

Stephen was with me at every show, selling tickets at the door, introducing me, recording the show, and running around with a second microphone for audience members. He also took bookings for private readings after the shows and, usually, booked the venues and organized advertising and posters for the shows.

My good friend Ingrid, who had had a son with her partner, Paul, not long before, invited Stephen and me to participate in the christening and naming ceremony in New Zealand, Paul's home country. Stephen and I decided to go, and when I mentioned the trip to Luke, he suggested that I stay on for another week and that he would come over to do some shows with me. Stephen agreed with the idea, but he needed to come back after the weekend to be with the kids. Stephen and I booked four shows, arranged accommodations, and organized advertising. We met Ingrid and Paul at their home in Sydney the night before our flight to New Zealand and boarded the flight together the next morning.

Paul's family met us when we had landed and drove us to their *marae*, or property with traditional buildings, including a big sacred building where everyone staying slept and prayed together and a separate building where they cooked and ate. As visitors, Stephen and I were required to be blessed by the head woman of Paul's family before we could step onto their sacred land. After that we had a lovely weekend experiencing New Zealand hospitality and the traditional naming ceremony and christening. In addition to Paul's family, we also met some of their friends, who had also travelled there for the weekend.

When the weekend was over, Stephen was dropped at the airport in Auckland and I was dropped at a motel. The next day I picked up the rental car Luke and I had organized, and went back to the motel. But then, in the underground car park there, I scraped the side of the rental car against the wall of the narrow driveway. I was really upset and not sure what I should do, so I called the rental company and told them about the damage. They requested that I bring the car back and get a replacement, but when I did that, the employee I saw explained to me that I had to pay the excess on the insurance, NZ$2,500, before I could hire another car. Luckily I had enough money to cover this, but it didn't leave me much and made the trip a lot more expensive. The whole experience was traumatic.

I left the damaged car there and caught a taxi to the Auckland airport to meet Luke. I told him what had happened, and we then caught another taxi to pick up the replacement car. I left all the driving to Luke after that. I also called Stephen to tell him what had happened, and he was upset for me and understanding, and he told me not to worry about it.

Our first show was the next day, but only twelve people came. Luke and I were a bit upset, as we had been hoping for more people. Nothing seemed to be going right.

The second show was in a town called Ottahungha a few hours' drive outside of Auckland, and we got there a bit late, just before the show was scheduled to start. People were everywhere when we arrived, and we sold eighty tickets. We were both much happier to attract that many people, and the show was great. It was after midnight when we arrived back at our motel.

The third show was at a place called Upper Hut near Wellington the next day. We got up early to leave, but we underestimated the travel time. After the very long drive from Auckland, we arrived thirty minutes after our show's planned start time. The club was sold out, although the room only seated fifty people. This show went really well despite the preshow drama, but then Luke lost his wallet with his share of the takings in it when he went to the bathroom before leaving, which was very frustrating. We stayed in a nearby motel that night, and the next day, we took our time driving back to Auckland as we had this day free.

Our last show was on Saturday night in a town called Papa Kura. Forty people turned up for it, and both Luke's readings and mine went well, but the week of shows had been very taxing on us both. On Sunday, we returned the rental car and went home. We were both happy to be finished with the tour. Because of the excess for the damage on the car, I came home with less money than I took, and I had missed Stephen and the kids. They were all waiting at the airport when we got back to Sydney, and I was so happy to see them.

After the trip, my business continued to grow, the kids were doing well at school, and Stephen and I were really happy, but my car broke down a lot, so it was time to get another one. I went online and found a cute little Peugeot convertible for a good price in a car yard in Sydney. I had some money saved but not enough, and I tried to organize a loan, but I hadn't been in business for long enough to satisfy the banks, so instead I told the car yard about my financial situation and asked them if I could purchase it by lay-by. The salesman agreed, so I put down my down payment, and after just a few months, I picked up my second-hand car, and Stephen and I sold the old one.

About six months after my first trip to New Zealand, I went back, as I had received a lot of requests to return. One lady who had been to our last show owned a small resort at Bethells Beach, and she arranged for me to do a small show there and three days of private readings. Luke didn't want to go back, so I took Stephen with me on this trip. We would be away for a week during the school holidays, so my kids stayed at Ian's and Eythan stayed at his nan's.

We also booked a show at Upper Hut and a couple of days of private readings there as well. The lady from Bethells Beach picked us up from the airport, and Stephen and I stayed at her resort for free. The show there attracted about forty people, and then after a couple of days of private readings, Stephen and I flew to Wellington, hired a car, and drove to Upper Hut. About forty people come to the second show as well, and several people at the show booked private readings for the days after. The whole trip went really well, and Stephen and I enjoyed the time together, even though I did have to work for most of it.

As time went on, we moved to a bigger home with a pool and a separate room at the back for readings and an adjacent sunroom that served as a waiting room. Having these areas separate from the house meant that they were a lot easier to keep tidy and clean, that I could leave them set up, and that the kids could stay home during my readings instead of having to go out. Not only that, but the house was also closer to the kids' school. This house made everything less stressful for the whole family, we all loved it, even the dogs.

It was now the end of 2010, I put down on my goals list for 2011 that I wanted to appear on television as a psychic medium, and just a few weeks later, in early January, I was contacted by a lady from a television show that had yet to air called *Psychic TV*. She was recruiting psychics to do readings on the show and she asked if I would like to audition to be a reader. I was thrilled at the opportunity and went down for the interview. There were four people conducting the interviews, which included the producer, director, host and the owner. They explained the intended format of the show and what was expected and I was required to do a reading for one of them to prove my ability. It would air a few days each week, and on each programme, psychics would do readings over the phone and would answer texts and voice messages live. I already had a busy schedule, but I made room to appear on the show once each week. On those days, I did readings all day and then travelled to Sydney, a two-hour trip from Cessnock, to appear on the show at night. Because the show started at 10:00 p.m. and I needed to be there thirty minutes before this, I left home at 7:30. The show then finished at 2:00 a.m., so I didn't arrive home until about 4:30. I needed the day off the next day to sleep, but as this was one of my two days off each week, I felt like I only had one day off. I did the show for about six months, but then the schedule affected my energy levels, so I needed to cut back on my appearances, and after nine months on the show, I stopped appearing altogether, although I've made occasional guest appearances since then.

During my time on *Psychic TV*, I finally decided to start my own Facebook account so people could connect with me through social networking. This has been very good for my profile and I now have thousands of friends. I also have a fan page with thousands of followers. I enjoy using Facebook, as I like to find beautiful pictures and positive quotes to post.

I also got myself a video camera so I could record some of my readings and shows, and I posted highlights from some of these on YouTube so that more people could see me in action and get an idea of how accurate my readings can be.

People from all over Australia and other countries were now contacting me for readings, which were booked out more than six months in advance, and people kept calling to make appointments. Stephen and I were doing great. We hardly ever had disagreements, and he continued to do so much for me, always complimenting, encouraging, and supporting to me, as well as being romantic. We talked about anything and everything and kept no secrets, and it seemed that not even our thoughts were secret. With the most amazing man in the world at my side, my life was really starting to get good.

Not long after I started at *Psychic TV,* I also started my own day-long course on psychic development and spiritual awareness. Stephen helped me put together a folder with all that day's course materials to give out to participants, helped me run the course, and also prepared the food for the day.

The course began with a talk from Stephen about meditation, chakras, and energy fields, and the group then did a meditation before breaking for morning tea. After this, I talked about mediumship and demonstrated bringing loved ones through from the other side. Then we broke for lunch. In the afternoon, I talked about psychometry, and all participants practiced using their abilities on each other. Stephen then talked about the Law of Attraction and how to use it. Finally, we broke for afternoon tea and finished the day talking about psychic tools, crystals, and angels, and I also demonstrated the use of tarot cards and palm reading. The course has run about twice a year since then, and I've had great feedback from all attendees.

Also in March this year it was announced that *The One: The Search for Australia's Most Gifted Psychic,* would have a second series and sought applications. Stephen was sure that not only would I get on but also that I'd win the competition. I sent in my application, which consisted of a number of psychic tests, and was then asked to come to Darling Harbour in Sydney for the next phase of selection. I was scheduled to appear on *Psychic TV* the night before, so I booked a motel to stay in Sydney. Stephen had to stay at home with the kids.

I got to bed just before 3:00 a.m. but was up at 9:00 to check out and go to Darling Harbour. I was still really tired and had some trouble finding the audition site and parking, which caused me a bit of stress. Then, I had to wait a few hours before I was called to audition. I had to do a five-minute reading for the interviewer. I had some real trouble connecting with her and didn't do a very good reading. I don't know if this was because of the lack of sleep, the stress, my nerves, or just the young lady's energy, but I left the interview thinking that I had blown it. A few days later it turned out that I had, as I was informed that I hadn't progressed to the next stage of auditions. I was upset that I hadn't made it onto the show, but I learnt from my mistakes and will be better prepared if I am ever given a similar chance in the future.

Around September, my mother and Gary decided to separate. Gary moved into a flat with a friend, and Mum prepared to move but had problems arranging suitable accommodation, so she asked if she could move in with Stephen, the kids, and me until she sorted something out. I talked to Stephen about this, and he was happy to have her for a while, even excited, as he thought it would be a good chance for him to get to know my mother better.

After about two weeks, Stephen and Mum seemed to be getting on fine, but then they had an argument and used some hurtful words. Mum decided it would be best for her to leave. I offered to pay for alternate accommodation until her new flat became available, and she arranged for Gary to pick her up the next day.

This was the only time Stephen and Mum had an argument. Stephen is normally very respectful, but he does have a temper and can be quite stubborn about his opinions, and so can Mum. At the time, these traits caused the disagreement to get out of hand.

However, Stephen forgave Mum and put the matter in the past. He knew how important family was to me and didn't want to cause any problems between my mum and me, and he never talked badly about my mum. He accepted her as she is, never complaining about her or my relationship with her, and he always encouraged me in it. I felt lucky to be with Stephen and could see both sides of the conflict between them. However, my mum did not forgive and hasn't seen or talked about Stephen since, and she doesn't like me or the kids to talk about him with her. I hope that one day Mum will forgive Stephen and put this behind her, and it would be great if she came to visit me again, as I don't get a lot of free time to visit her.

Countless times, Stephen has come home and said, "Guess what!" to test if I can pick up what he wants to tell me or what he has to give me or plans to get for me. I almost always guess his news, it's surprising to think about how many times I've been able to do this. I do still get surprised by gifts, but the surprise comes before I have the actual gift.

At other times, Stephen has gone out without telling me where, but I've known where to call if I needed to contact him, as he doesn't carry a mobile phone. Once, I called his friend's house while he was there because I needed him to get something from the shops, and he said, "How did you know I was here?" I told him I just knew, and then he asked, "Did you try anywhere else first?"

I said, "No, my guides told me you were there!" He was amazed.

Another time, Stephen returned from being out, and I said, "You've been to Dave's, haven't you?"

A big smile came to his face, and he said, "No I haven't"

"Are you sure?" I said, as my guides had told me that he had. He repeated that he hadn't been to Dave's, and I felt a bit confused, so I went into another room. Then it hit me: I had mixed up which friend's place he had been to. I yelled out, "Not Dave, I meant Brian! You've been at Brian's!" He yelled back from the other room that I was right. For a moment he had thought he had me, but my guides seldom let me down. He often jokes that he'd never be able to cheat on me because I would know and would stop him before anything even started.

The kids can never get away with anything, either. Once, I heard Jacob ask Stephen if he could go for a walk, and when Stephen asked him where he planned to go, Jacob said, "Oh, nowhere, really. I just wanted to go for a walk."

I then said, "You're planning to walk to McDonalds to buy a sundae with your pocket money, aren't you?"

He dropped his head and said yes in a soft voice. He was only ten and McDonalds was located on a main road about a twenty minute walk from home. Also he was trying to be sneaky, so he wasn't allowed to go.

Picking up things like this from my guides, and sometimes from spirits, too, has been a really good thing, as they help me a lot in my day-to-day life. My kids get frustrated with it, but Stephen likes that I can do this, as he says that just knowing they're around is very comforting. Nan and other spirits connected to me often appear in my dreams, and although I don't see them when I'm awake, I can feel them near. My guides are always popping in and out at any time of day, with information for me, I know each one by their feel, and occasionally I will see them.

Since Stephen and I had been together, we had totally changed our lives around. We now had enough money to live comfortably and pay down our debts. We've even been able to afford many little getaways together and with the children, including a ten-day cruise around the New Caledonia islands. The kids, too, had become happy and settled, and our relationship was strong and stable. Stephen and I made many plans for our future, including owning a spiritual retreat and health centre. We maintained a good balance of work and play, taking time to relax when we could. Our life continues to get better and better. It has been like a fairy tale; together, we have found our own little piece of heaven on earth.

Chapter 5

Reaching for the Stars

At the end of 2011, I had been doing a few shows with some other mediums, and one of them suggested that we travel to do shows and readings in the UK together. I was all for it, and we all agreed, so we set a date for June 2012. We all thought we should be able to go and I saved my money, and as I would be gone for four weeks, Stephen and I decided that it would be best for the children and our expenses for him to stay home. I enquired about a working visa, but it turned out that because both of my parents were born in the UK, I was eligible for dual citizenship in that country, so I arranged for that and a UK passport. Then, about two months before the trip, the other mediums pulled out because they had had trouble saving money for it. We hadn't yet booked anything, but I had put aside the time for the trip and had saved the money I needed, so I decided to go on my own.

My friend Nova, a producer for *Psychic TV* who had returned home to the UK after the show was up and running, invited me to stay with her family during the tour and offered to line up some psychic shows for me. Sue, a lady in the UK whom I knew through Facebook, organized shows and fairs for psychics in the UK was also happy to book some for me as well. Things were falling into place, and I felt much more relaxed knowing that people were helping to book some work for me.

I then bought my plane tickets and sorted out my itinerary. Nova was very busy with work and was not able to organize any shows for me, but she insisted that I stay with her for a few days to do some sightseeing and catching up, and I decided that was a good idea. I planned my first three days in London and the following four days with Nova, giving me the first week to relax and see the sights.

Sue, on the other hand, had arranged four shows, two psychic fairs, and some private readings for me. For the first show, in Ellesmere, Shropshire, she had also booked Colin Fry, and all 160 tickets had already sold out. Colin had agreed to let me come on before him and perform for thirty minutes. I was absolutely thrilled about this, as Colin was famous in the UK for doing readings on his own TV show and on other shows. I had also read his books and seen him in action on TV before. The other three shows also featured Carl Mann, Jan Harris, and Greg Smith, all of whom were good mediums, but none of these other shows sold out. I also planned to do platform work at a few spiritualist churches and readings at psychic fairs and in people's homes. This would keep me quite busy for the other three weeks that I was there.

I spent the first couple of days in London visiting Stonehenge, the roman Baths, St. Paul's Cathedral, Windsor Castle, and many other famous sites. Then I travelled by train to Birmingham to stay with Nova's family, during my stay, I hired a car and visited the house where Nan grew up and other important sites. Before I had left Australia, I had had some difficulty uploading a UK map onto my GPS device, so I left it behind while Stephen worked it out, and he posted it to Nova's address. However, it didn't arrive before I left Nova's, so I had to struggle with road maps, which I have never been good at following.

On the night of my first show, with Colin Fry, I got lost on the way to the venue and arrived only just in time. I didn't have time to meditate and ground myself before I had to perform. I was stressed out and nervous, and it took a little while to get settled onstage, but in the end, I did some good readings, and then was able to relax and watch Colin perform. All up, it was a good night, and I was very proud of myself. Colin seemed like a lovely man and was very talented and funny onstage.

On the way back to the bed and breakfast where I was staying, I was tired and unfamiliar with the roads, which were very narrow compared to what I was used to in Australia, and when I was about to turn into the driveway at the B & B, a car behind me beeped its horn as it over took me, which distracted me and caused me to scrape the side of the car on the stone gate. The damage to the car wasn't too bad, but the next evening, I did the same thing again, which made the damage much worse.

During the trip, I talked to Stephen every day on the phone or on Skype and told him everything. Time seemed so slow, and I missed Stephen, the kids, and home so much that I wanted to leave, but I had work booked and had to honour my commitments, so I stuck it out.

The rest of my visit was without incident. I did the shows and fairs and picked up a few private readings, but I didn't make much money from these, and with my expenses, that money dwindled down almost to nothing. Stephen had to borrow some money from a friend and deposit it into my account so that I had enough to last the rest of the trip.

When I returned the rental car at the airport, I explained the damage and was told I needed to pay the 800-pound excess, or about 1,500 Australian dollars, which I did not have, so I filled out some paperwork so the company could send me the bill. The computers were playing up and the office was quite busy, so the clerk put my paperwork aside to sort out later and let me go. My angels must have been looking after me that day, as I never heard anything more from the company, and I was grateful.

Stephen and the kids were waiting for me at the Sydney airport when I arrived. I was so happy to be back. Being on my own in a strange place had taken its toll on me. I was exhausted, and my legs had swollen painfully during the flight, so I had to stay in bed until the swelling went down a couple days later. The trip brought up a lot of emotions from when I had to deal with everything on my own, and my depression and anxiety returned, and they were intense, and so did my headaches. I had to reschedule quite a few readings, as I wasn't well enough to do them on their scheduled days.

Over the next few months, Stephen helped me deal with my issues, and I also saw a counsellor again and tried hypnotherapy, all of which helped a little but not as much as I needed them to. I saw my doctor and a specialist, and they changed my medication, which also helped. Finally, I settled down, and my emotions improved, which was such a relief.

Over the years, I'd tried many types of healing and underwent many treatments, to aid my depression and anxiety, and to help me feel balanced and relaxed, including past-life regression sessions, hypnotism, reiki healing, theta healing, sound healing, energy healing, crystal healing, massage therapy, and beauty treatments. Because I'm so sensitive, being so aware of my energy has allowed me to experience some amazing things during some of these healing sessions. I've seen angels and spirit guides standing over me working on my energy with the healer, on a few occasions I've spoken in languages that I don't know, and at times I've felt bolts of energy shoot through my body. I love having healing work done on me, and I always take something away from each session.

The most amazing treatment I've ever had was done by my good friend Greg, who lives and works in Lithgow in the Blue Mountains, where I often did psychic readings and shows. I met him not long after I first started going to Lithgow in 2008 as he was doing healing work at the place where I was doing readings. He worked with crystals and energies and higher powers to move energy through a client's body, and he did a session on me. This was amazing, and every time I saw him after that, I wanted another healing session.

On one visit to Greg's house, in 2012, his healing on me blew me away. By working with his crystals and connecting to divine spirits, bolts of energy came through his hands and into each area of my body that needed healing. The love he used from only the highest of the highest intention and his deep connection to the entities and spirits brought me into a deep meditative state. I felt total bliss, love, and gratitude for the spirit beings that presented themselves in the room. One of the spirit guides communicated with me through telepathy, telling me that his name was Ekertate. He looked like a monk in his cloak and hood, and I felt that he was a highly evolved spirit guide. Ekertate walked around the room, keeping a very close eye on Greg. I also saw an image of my higher self, standing behind me, I saw other beings in the room watching the session. I felt like I was floating.

Afterwards, I felt like my spirit had left my body and hadn't fully returned, and my muscles were so relaxed that I couldn't sit up or even walk without help. It took more than an hour of sitting and relaxing for my strength to fully return. I felt very calm and peaceful for weeks after the healing and stronger emotionally, like a weight had been lifted, giving me more inner power. I had never experienced anything like this before.

At the end of 2012, when Stephen and I were setting our goals for 2013, we discussed adding writing and publishing my book to the list and agreed that it was time to start it. A woman named Sue who had come to one of our courses had mentioned to me that she had just completed a graphic art course at Tafe, and that if I was ever thinking of making my own deck of guidance cards, she would love to be involved. She then followed up just before Christmas, and Stephen and I had discussed it, and I decided to go ahead with the project. I also felt ready for doing something new on television, so I put this on my list as well. Stephen and I also put building our own spiritual retreat centre down as a long-term goal and planned in some detail what we would like.

Stephen and I then started 2013 with all guns blazing. We invited Sue over for dinner to discuss our ideas about the cards and see what she was able to do for the artwork. I described what I wanted each card to look like, and Sue told us that it would probably take us at least six months to complete the work. We got started.

I sat and wrote my book and the cards' meanings to go in the pamphlet, regularly. I sat in my reading room and meditated on each card, and then I wrote down what I wanted the meaning to say. Stephen then edited these so that people could understand each message. I took my time on these, as I felt there was no rush, and the book often took priority, as it was a much bigger task.

I worked on the book in the evenings if I had the energy and tried to put time aside on at least one of my days off for writing. Stephen then went over what I had written and suggested changes, and I asked him to make them for me. One of the hardest parts was trying to remember details from the past. Stephen and I remembered our few years together slightly differently, which had us both second-guessing our memories. It was much easier to write the chapters in which I share my knowledge than those in which I discuss the events from my life.

Because the book took a lot of time, we couldn't give the cards as much attention as we wanted to. Sue explained that she needed a lot more input from us, as the art work on the first few cards she showed us were not quite what we had imagined, but she lived far away, which made it hard to meet with her to discuss the project, so Stephen and I decided to put the cards on hold until after the book was finished. I plan to complete them in 2014.

In February 2013, I noticed a post on Facebook by Simon Turnbull, the head of the Australian Psychic Association, that said that Haunted Australia, an investigative team, were looking for a psychic medium to assist in their investigations. I had a quick look at their website and decided to call them. I told Kade, the business's owner, a bit about myself, and he asked me to send him a bio and said he would let me know if we could work together in the next day or two. The next day, Kade called me back, and he seemed impressed with my bio and asked if I could attend an investigation that Sunday. He also explained that I wouldn't be paid for my work and that I had to pay my own expenses, but it did offer new experiences and more exposure in my industry, so I decided to do it.

Kade and his wife, Lara, put together a team of people dedicated to providing tangible evidence of paranormal activity with pictures, video footage from special cameras, and recordings of everything that happens in each investigation. The team researches each place they visit before they arrive, and once on site, they set up a variety of technical equipment, including infrared cameras and those with infrablue filters, connect them to computers, and wait to capture anything that shows up. Kade is very professional in his approach to his work and very dedicated to it, and he also plans to put together a series of episodes for television.

That Sunday, Stephen came with me to the investigation in the Southern Highlands, about a four-hour drive from Cessnock. I was scheduled to be there at 3:00 p.m., but we arrived at about 4:00, so I missed out on the talk about the investigation site and the equipment set-up. As soon as we arrived, I was taken straight into a walk-through of the site, a former orphanage. Kade and a few team members with cameras and other equipment followed me and recorded what I could pick up. In each area, Kade narrated and talked a little on camera and then asked me what I sensed.

I picked up on spirits straight away. One was a boy of about fifteen years old who told me that his name was Kenny. He was about five feet eight inches tall and had red hair and freckles. He told me he had been a ward of the state since he was five and that he tried to protect younger kids from the bullies and the violent and abusive workers, like a big brother. He often took the blame, and therefore the punishment, for what the other children did so they wouldn't be hurt. He showed me images of his being tied up and whipped, and he said that he had been shot one night and his body buried somewhere on the property.

I saw a tall man who looked like a warden carrying a lot of keys that rattled as he walked up and down the corridors. I also saw children who told me about evil men they feared. I sensed a lot of cruelty and abuse, including sexual abuse.

As I walked through the site, at times I became overwhelmed with emotion and sick to my stomach because of the abuse these poor children suffered. Most of the children were boys and had become wards of the state by no fault of their own. Kenny told me of a room called the boiler room where the children would be locked up and left on their own in the dark for days. There, the evil men tied them up, and stripped them, beat them, and raped them.

In a room downstairs, I saw a spirit man who had dark hair, a skinny body, and missing teeth at the front of his mouth. He yelled, "Get out!" and gave me a fright, after which I had an eerie feeling. Then one of the spirit children said he was one of the evil men who had hurt them when he was alive.

Next, I saw a spirit wearing a white lab coat who put the children in straitjackets and heavily sedated them when they cried and screamed and then often left them for dead. I also picked up on a girl of about ten years who had died when she jumped from the top balcony. She had tried to kill herself previously by slitting her wrists because she was traumatized after being raped and depressed because of the conditions she had been subjected to.

I felt that the place had been run a like a military prison because of the strict discipline to the children. I saw images in my mind of children walking along with their heads down and their hands tied behind their backs and of the evil men running the place playing games by throwing homemade fire bombs at the children and shooting their guns near them to make them run and to terrify them. These poor, innocent spirit children said that they wanted the truth to come out. I felt blessed and honoured that the children entrusted me with this information about their ordeal.

After my walk-through, Kade then interviewed some of the people who currently worked at the establishment. I sat at the back of the room and listened while Kade filmed each interview. The employees described taps turning themselves on, doors opening or slamming closed, and thinking they saw someone when no one else was there. One person told us that a spirit had pushed him down the stairs and that he had experienced other paranormal activity whilst working.

Then, a cleaner told Kade and the team that forty-five years before, she had been a ward of the state herself and had actually stayed at this orphanage when she was about eight years old. She described a young boy named Kenny with red hair who tried to protect the other children from the workers. She confirmed everything that I had said about him, even that he had been shot! She said that his death was supposedly an accident when the guard fired a warning shot that hit him and that the official story was that he went missing, and his death wasn't reported at the time. There was only one documented death at this site where a young boy was killed by a falling branch from a tree. There were no other documented deaths at this location however the spirit children had told me there had been a lot of deaths and many unmarked graves throughout the property and so much abuse and torture they were subjected to on a daily basis. The cleaner also told Kade that she knew of a few children who died there but there deaths were never reported and always covered up by the people running the place at the time.

Kade was amazed and repeatedly looked at me as this lady verified what I had said, and after this interview, he said he was impressed by what I had picked up. He said that he had spent a lot of money on equipment to gather evidence of spirits and had spent many hours researching everything he could about the investigation site, but I had walked in without any of that and was able to tell him things he had learnt in his research and a lot more that he hadn't known. He asked if I was willing to do more work with him. I had found the evening really informative, and I was proud of the work I had done, so I said yes.

The next day Kade emailed me dates for all of Haunted Australia's upcoming investigations and said that he wanted me to participate in as many as I could manage. He also asked my permission to list me as the team's main medium on their website and Facebook page, making any other mediums they worked with when I was unavailable, guest mediums. I was thrilled and said yes. Stephen and I then worked to reschedule some of my bookings to accommodate the investigations and then let Kade know the dates I was available. Since then, I've felt blessed to be a part of this team and have really enjoyed the investigations.

The week after Simon Turnbull posted about the opening with Haunted Australia on Facebook, he posted about an upcoming TV competition show for experienced stage mediums a prize of $250,000 for the winner and gave contact information for Dean, the shows producer. I didn't give the prize money any consideration but thought that it may be good exposure, so I called Dean to get some more information. We talked for about ten minutes, and he asked me questions about what I did and what experience I had, and then he said he would forward some information to me.

The email I received was not what I expected. The show was *Australia's Got Talent*, and the producers wanted mediums to compete against singers, dancers, comedians, and performers with other talents. I thought straight away that there was no way a medium would win, but because of the potential for exposure, I decided to give it a go.

Dean asked me to consider ways to make my act more exciting as I progressed through each round of the competition if I was successful and to tell him of any special requirements I had. I asked him to organize a person with someone close in spirit who was open to having a mediumship reading done. I then suggested a number of ways to make my act more exciting: doing a reading by holding something that belonged to the person I was reading for instead of having the person onstage, doing readings for two people at the same time, doing a reading for someone I selected from the audience, and even reading for a sceptic, who are always hard to read for, as they have so many walls up and don't accept general information as psychic messages. Dean agreed to organize a crew member for a reading during the audition and said he was impressed that I had given the act so much thought.

A few weeks later, Dean informed me of what time to show up for my audition and that I would have two minutes to perform not in front of the judges and audience but for a few people in a room where I could be interviewed. This was a big relief and made me much more comfortable about my first audition.

On the day of the audition, Stephen, Shaylee, and I went to the Newcastle Town Hall, where the auditions were being held. When we arrived, I registered my act, and the young lady at the counter was very nice and bubbly and interested in what I did. She said she had never had a reading before but was open to having one done. I explained that I was booked out until the following year but that today I'd be reading for a crew member I didn't know. Stephen, Shaylee, and I then took a seat and waited for almost two hours before I was called up to do my act.

I was taken into a room to meet a man who was going to interview me, a lady behind a camera, and the young lady from the registration desk, who had talked someone into letting her be the person whose reading I'd do.

I then took a seat, and the man asked me questions about me and what I do, and then I began my two-minute reading. The lady was quite young, and I didn't pick up on any spirits around her, as she may not have had anyone close to her pass away. I asked my guides for some help and then told her what I picked up about her life and events that had happened in her recent past. I didn't stop to let her speak, as I had limited time. but I knew I was getting things right, as she nodded and her eyes went wide a few times. After my time was up, I stopped, and the camera operator recorded the young lady's response.

She was blown away. Everything I said had been spot on, and the details I gave totally took her by surprise. Then the interviewer asked me if I could pick up on anything for him, and I described his apartment and his partner and said that they had been discussing adopting a child. He was also amazed, although his response was not recorded, and then the lady behind the camera asked if I could pick up anything for her. I picked up that she had recently had a car accident that had greatly upset her, and I described the car and how the accident had happened.

I walked out of the room almost thirty minutes after I had gone in. As the young lady opened the door for me, she said to my daughter, who was waiting outside, "Your mum is amazing." My daughter said, "I know." I was so happy with how the audition had gone and felt quietly confident that I would make it through to the theatre auditions in Sydney. I would have to wait seven weeks to find out if I had made it through, so I went home and back to business as usual.

When the date of the announcement arrived, I wasn't contacted. I was a little surprised, given how impressed the people I had read for were during the audition. However, I knew that they had their reasons not to pick me, and I was happy that I had been able to put myself out there and do a good job. I had impressed myself by having the courage to face my fears and anxieties, regardless of the outcome.

About halfway through 2013, Jacob asked to talk to me, and I knew straight away what he wanted to talk about: moving in with his father. Jacob wasn't surprised that I knew before he said anything. I told him that it would be best to discuss the matter as a family, so Stephen, Shaylee, and I sat down with him to talk. I was sad that I wouldn't be able to see him as often if he moved but I was okay with it, as I knew he loved his dad and wanted to spend more time with him. We discussed all of his options, and then we called Ian, and he said he was okay with the idea too. We then made arrangements with Jacob's school, and he moved to the Blue Mountains to live with Blake and his dad. I missed having Jacob with us, but I knew he was fine with his dad, and I still got to see him and talk to him on the phone often. I am so proud of Jacob. He went through so much with his ADHD, but he has settled down and become a well-rounded young man with a good head on his shoulders and a gentle, loving heart. I trust him and know he is happy and secure with his father.

Then, in August, the Australian Psychic Association held its thirtieth anniversary dinner in Sydney, which also marked a transition for them, as they had changed their name from the Australian Psychic Association to the International Psychic Association because of the addition of many international psychics. Hundreds of psychics from all around Australia would come together under one roof for this special event, and I didn't want to miss out, so I purchased tickets for Stephen and me. A week or two before the date, we were informed that the dinner was being filmed for a TV documentary, and then Simon told me that the filmmakers wanted to interview a number of psychics and had asked if I would be one of the sixteen psychics to be interviewed. I was so excited and was honoured to have been asked. Simon conducted the interview, asking me questions about my abilities and having me tell stories from my past. The documentary is scheduled to air in 2015.

On the night of the anniversary dinner, Stephen and I stayed in Sydney. More than two hundred people attended, including many big names in the industry. I had met a few of them through Facebook, including Mitchell Coombes, who came straight over to say hello as soon as he saw me, which was really nice. We had met once before at one of his shows, but we had connected well, as we had so much in common. Stephen and I then went inside, found our table, and then saw who was there. I said hi and had little chats with people I knew and introduced myself to others. I was quite surprised to find everyone seemed to know who I was, even the award-winning psychics, and people told me they had heard good things about me. It was a massive compliment to be recognized, as it meant that I had made an impact on the industry, even though I hadn't yet won any awards or been on any big TV shows. Learning that my reputation had grown even without that exposure enough for top psychics there to treat me as an equal made me feel like one of the most successful people there.

I had many conversations, met some really lovely, talented people, and made some wonderful connections with like-minded people. The energy was positive, and everyone had a great time. I look forward to the next big dinner with the IPA. I feel that one day I'll accept an award from the association, although I realize that I don't need awards to be successful or to be noticed.

I continue to grow personally, and my business continues to expand with more psychic shows and readings booked out over a year in advance. I am still working with Haunted Australia around the country as they film their TV series. I also teach people about what I do and show them how to develop their own abilities, and I am constantly learning and growing as a person and as a psychic. I continue to take courses, read books, and listen to podcasts to help me develop. I am very happy with my life, and I am driven to achieve success in my business as a psychic medium. I also still have dreams to record my music, including making an album of spiritual songs, and feel confident that I'll do well with this when the time is right. I also still dream of being on TV, and I feel sure that before too long, many people will see me on more TV programmes. I also dream of building a spiritual retreat when I have enough money.

I see myself as being on my way up as I improve my life. I face my fears and anxieties every day, and although they will always be there, no longer are they debilitating. I do my best to honour my walk with others. I am not yet the person I want to be, but I grow and learn more every day, and although I am still fragile and sensitive, I am now much stronger than I have ever been. I've been through a lot, but as a psychic medium, I can see and feel how much other people have endured, and what I've faced seems small in comparison. Life can be difficult, but I know that if I put my mind to something and apply it in the right way, I can create my own reality. The more I focus on positive things, the more positive things I attract into my life.

Chapter 6

My Thoughts and Beliefs

As a psychic medium, I believe that I have insight into what happens when we pass over after our death and that I have a good understanding of many spiritual matters and life in general. In this chapter, I share what I believe is true at this time in my life in hope that you'll gain some insights that help you on your journey through life.

As a free-willed person, I may change my views, and I understand that others are quite passionate about beliefs that differ. I cannot tell you what to believe, as you have to decide what is true for you, and I respect those beliefs. I ask that you also respect my right to choose what I believe.

When I was a teenager, I started to read about spirituality and religion, including the Bible and books about Buddhism, Hinduism, and any other belief system I could find. I have also read about palmistry, tarot cards, numerology, spirits, angels, and psychic abilities. There are too many to list, but the following are a few of my favourites: *The Power of Now* by Eckhart Tolle, The Celestine Prophecy series by James Redfield, *Realms of the Earth Angels* and *Angel Therapy* by Doreen Virtue, *Anatomy of the Spirit* by Caroline Myss, *Spirit Release* by Sue Allen, *Journey of the Soul* by Michael Newton, *Ask Your Guides* and *Trust Your Vibes* by Sonia Choquette, *Personal Power through Awareness* and *Spiritual Growth: Being Your Higher Self* by Sanaya Roman, and *Saved by Angels* by Glennyce Eckersley.

I have also read books written by famous psychics, including John Edward, Edgar Kayce, Colin Fry, Tony Stockwell, Lisa Williams, and Doris Stokes.

To gain a better understanding of myself, to improve my life, and to overcome depression, anxiety, and some of the trials I have faced, I've read motivational and self-improvement books, especially *The Secret*, *The Law of Attraction*, *The Vortex*, and *Ask and It Is Given* by Esther Hicks; *Think and Grow Rich* by Napoleon Hill; *Millionaire Messenger* by Brendon Burchard; *Affirmations* by Stuart Wilde; and *You Can Do It: Believe and Achieve* by Paul Hanna.

I have also attended countless courses and seminars, including those on tarot, reiki, ThetaHealing, igniting your spirit, the inner child, advanced psychic development, Wiccan development, parenting, wealth building, the power of the mind, and dozens more on other spiritual and self-help topics.

I have listened to cassettes, CDs, and podcasts on self-motivation and spirituality, learning from and being inspired by great people, including Wayne Dyer, Eckhart Tolle, Esther Hicks, Doreen Virtue, Louise Hay, Maryanne Williamson, Deepak Chopra, Oprah Winfrey, Paul McCormick, Brendon Burchard, Tony Robbins, Suze Orman, Bob Proctor, and Zig Ziglar. I like to listen to these when I'm driving or relaxing at home, as I enjoy using times that would otherwise be wasted for learning.

Besides reading and listening to experts, I've also gained knowledge from talking to people I've met in my everyday life, and even people's status and comments on Facebook have given me insights into many subjects. My psychic abilities also give me a unique insight into other people's lives. I get to learn much more about people I do readings for than most people could from speaking to the same people, and I often feel their suffering. I'm blessed that I can connect with people in this way. I believe my abilities have given me a better understanding of people in general and have helped me to be more compassionate, more respectful, more tolerant, and more accepting of others. I am also humbled, even in awe, when I see and feel the difficulties other people have overcome. I know that no one is perfect and that no one has all the answers.

Although we might see the same thing, our different perspectives often cause us to perceive it completely differently. We continuously change how we view ourselves and the world around us, depending on our energies, our circumstances, our states of mind, and outside influences. The opinions and experiences of others, especially those we know and trust, shape our own. However, only you can choose what you think and believe. Just because someone says skydiving is fantastic doesn't mean you'll like the experience. Just because someone doesn't like someone, it doesn't mean you'll not like that person. Just because someone believes in God doesn't mean that you have to. Just because someone is on a certain path doesn't mean you have to follow. Be open as you listen to what others have to say, as when we are open to listening, we can see things from new angles and gain a better understanding of them, but make up your own mind.

A Word on Giving Advice

I believe that it is good to share our knowledge and life experiences to help others grow and learn. We can give advice based on our experiences or our feelings. We must remember that another person does not have to take our advice; but that advice may help him or her understand something better and help him or her to make a more informed decision.

Not all advice is good and not all is bad; it just is. It is up to us all to take or disregard any information as we feel it is right for us. However, if you don't express yourself and share your opinion, you deny both yourself and others an opportunity to grow. Always think carefully about any advice you give, and always offer it as something that another person *may consider*, not what he or she *should* or *should not* do, as multitudes of options are always available to us all, and what works for one person doesn't always work for another.

Clients often ask me for advice, and sometimes the choices are obvious and simple and it is easy to advise them, but other times the choices may have major life-changing consequences. In these cases, giving advice can be tricky, so I may suggest that they think the decision through logically and not let their emotions cloud their judgement, asking themselves, what they really want, what they feel is the best choice for them, and how their choice might affect others in their lives. I may also suggest that they meditate and ask their own guides and angels for guidance. Often, these people have already made their choices and only want my confirmation that they have made the correct choice. Sometimes I see with my psychic abilities, the choices people will make and tell them that they'll make them regardless of any advice they've been given. It is not up to me to say whether that choice is the best or the correct choice to make, and any choice that any of us make has positive and negative consequences, so whether it's right depends on what we focus on.

Remember also to listen to the advice you give to others, as it may be advice that you need to hear as well.

Being Happy

Living a happy, resilient, and optimistic life is wonderful for your health, as it protects you from the stresses of life. Stress is linked to heart disease, cancer, and stroke, leading causes of death. Unfortunately, many people look outside themselves for things to make them feel happy, whether they be material possessions, other people, certain places. These people confuse enjoyment with happiness. Enjoyment is something we gain from the outside from things like chocolate, shopping, swimming, or relaxing, and this enjoyment may lead to happiness, but it may not. If we eat too much chocolate, we can make ourselves feel sick or gain weight; if we go shopping in a crowded shopping centre, we may get frustrated finding parking or waiting in line; if we choose to go swimming and when the water is too cold or dirty, we may get sick; and so on. Anything can happen to make the otherwise enjoyable experience unpleasant and make us unhappy. Whatever you feel makes you happy today may not make you happy tomorrow, as circumstances change.

Happiness is a choice. By looking at the positives in any situation and letting go of the negatives, we can stay happy. It is hard to feel happy if you're constantly complaining, so don't complain, and be aware of how your thoughts and your words affect you. The emotions you feed become the biggest. If you feed, or focus on negative emotions more than the positive ones, then you can't expect to feel happy. When you learn to accept the negative without dwelling on it and to always look for the positive, you'll notice that you feel happy more often.

In this way, true happiness comes from within, and you can feel happy at any time you choose to. You can feel happy just by thinking about things that make you happy. Happiness is always inside you. To feel it, simply choose to appreciate all the good things in your life and look for things to be grateful for, as when we feel gratitude and appreciation, we feel happiness as a side effect. The more you feel grateful for and the more you appreciate, the happier you will be.

Judgement

As a spiritualist, I'm told not to judge others, but I've found this is a very hard thing to do! People naturally form opinions on everything and anything. Our opinions are shaped by our experiences, our beliefs, our upbringing, our friends, our communities, and society as a whole. Our current state of mind also plays a major role in any opinions we form. These opinions and judgements can be positive or negative.

When we form an opinion, we make a judgement. In my opinion, there is nothing wrong with forming opinions and making judgements on anything. It is a necessity of life!

The actual act of making a judgement is not a problem; a problem arises only when we try to force that opinion or judgement onto others, as we do when we put others down because of our judgements or ridicule others because our opinions differ. This causes conflict. Instead, we must respect other people's right to have their own opinions and beliefs.

Having said this, however, we all should respect and uphold some basic human rights. When people's actions violate these basic human rights, they may be punished, but that punishment often does not stop them from repeating their actions. Rather than being punished, they should be educated so that they change the way they think and behave.

The trick is not to not judge but not to take on the judgements of others, or to let them go. Don't adopt others' opinions unless you've formed the same opinion on your own. We can express our opinions all we like, and we should allow others to choose to agree or disagree with them.

We are all teachers and students of life. As we grow, we help others to grow as well. We all need to show respect for others and for ourselves. Let go of others' opinions that don't resonate with your own truth. What they think is theirs to think and belongs to them; if you know what is true for you, then it is of no concern to you that someone else believes differently. If some don't see the light you shine, that only means they're looking elsewhere.

Outside influences affect us and often others can't see these. When someone is being negative, it is often a reflection of their circumstances, and is not up to us to judge those actions or expressions, for we can't see the whole picture of their lives. I always try to send positive energy to people when they act negatively towards me, for it is at these times that they most need love, compassion, and understanding. When we realize we are all beautiful when we're at our best and that this beauty is always within us, it is easier to bring that out in others. If you always speak and act with kindness from a loving heart, than that is what will come back to you.

Everything just is; it is both, good and bad, positive and negative. When you allow yourself to see the many sides to everything, then you can accept it all and remain balanced.

Arguments, Disagreements, and Conflicts

We can very easily get caught up in an argument or disagreement with others, as we all have our own opinions and viewpoints. What one person thinks is right another person may think is wrong. All too often we go on the defensive. If someone says or does something that we take offense to or that makes us feel attacked, we all too often react by reflecting that person's negative energy. What starts out as a minor disagreement can suddenly be blown way out of proportion, and we can say things that we don't really mean. We also tend to read things into what others say that aren't there, and we make assumptions. We also revert to childish behaviour instead of acting like adults. All of this can break friendships lead to bitterness and anger that lasts as long as we want them too. We all instinctively act like this, but we don't have to; we always have a choice. We are capable of stepping back and thinking before we act or react allowing us to respond positively instead.

If we let go of our hurt and respond with love, compassion, and understanding, then we can avoid so much conflict and all the negative consequences that come with it. You don't have to agree with another person; you can choose to accept his or her point of view as different from yours, understanding that it is his or her choice to believe this way and your choice to believe differently.

Next time you feel you're being attacked, step back and respond from love, leaving all negativity out of your response.

You don't have to change your energy to match anyone else's. You have choices. The way I see it is simple, really: Everything is energy. We are energy, so our thoughts, words, and actions are also energy. Quantum physics teaches us that when two energies vibrating at different frequencies come together, either one of the energies will change to match the frequency of the other or the energies will repel each other.

When someone is putting out negative energy, regardless of the type of energy it is, you can choose whether you allow that energy to change your own energy, or you can repel it. For example, if someone is complaining, we can allow it to cause us to vibrate at the same frequency by not fully processing the complaint properly, and then we reflect that same energy, agreeing with the complaint or complaining ourselves.

Or we can choose to remain neutral and repel the negative energy, or you can put out positive energy that is stronger than the negative energy of the other person and influence the other person to match your positivity. You can choose to not respond to the person's complaint or by finding the positive side to the complaint.

The more you look for positivity, the easier it is to find. You may try gently asking a complainer why he feels that way or why he is letting a situation affect him in this way. This may make him stop, think about the situation, and then respond rather than react. When we show understanding, it is easier to persuade others to look at their circumstances differently.

If someone pushes your buttons and you can't respond from love, then walk away, even if only to let the air clear and to settle down. Don't let your negative thoughts fester and become negative actions. To do so, be willing to forgive, even when you feel that someone else is in the wrong. Holding grudges only does you harm, not those against whom you hold grudges. We all need to learn to accept that we are all different and that those differences should be respected.

Regardless of your background, religion or faith or lack thereof, you can choose to be respectful or rude in any discussion. When someone puts down another for his or her beliefs, regardless of what they are, this is rude and disrespectful and shows much more about the person attacking than the person he or she attacks. Further, reacting with the same rudeness only creates conflict. Before responding, ask yourself if you are responding respectfully. We can easily justify our own actions when we try, but no one really wins in conflict. To have faith is to believe without proof, so it is pointless to quote or to present other evidence to someone who is not open to changing his or her faith. I don't see things as being black or white or right or wrong, but I can see things as positive and negative, and I would prefer to take on the positive and let the negative go. My spiritual faith is mine and is defined by my understanding of many things, it is as definite to me as love is. Others may consider it fanciful or even wrong, but that is not my concern.

To make a point in a more understanding way, you can use more compassion or you can word your point differently. I always try to speak and respond with a kind heart and positive energy, but when I express my opinion, I know that I can't change those of others; it's hard enough to make changes within myself. I try to accept others as they are, and if their energy is vibrating differently than mine, then I remind myself that I won't need to put up with them for long, as I am free to choose for myself.

I am a big believer of the saying, "If you can't say anything nice, then don't say anything at all." Saying something that has the potential to hurt someone else's feelings or upset them is often not worth saying, as most people will take negative comments personally and react negatively. I prefer to not seek out conflict in this way.

Always remember what other people think, even if it is about you, is theirs and has nothing to do with you, and it will only affect you if you allow it to.

Forgiveness

Forgiveness frees a person emotionally, spiritually, and even physically, and many common sayings about forgiveness, such as "It is always better to forgive and forget" and "To forgive is divine," reflect its benefits. But as we all know; to speak of forgiveness is one thing, but to practise it is completely different. Why should we forgive if we still feel upset or angry when we have been used, abused, betrayed, insulted, embarrassed, belittled, disrespected, or hurt?

When we have a problem with someone about something we value, then we can become angry or upset with that person. Our emotions create our feelings, and when emotions stir up negative feelings, we often hold on to these feelings for a long time. This can happen whether the problem is real or imagined—that is, when we can hold someone responsible for something when it is not their fault but we've assumed or jumped to the conclusion that it is, blaming the other person for creating the problem and upsetting us. Many of us hold on to feelings about circumstances in our childhood or in past relationships, and these affect not just us but those around us. When people fall off the horse so to speak, some will put this behind them and get back on but others will hold on to the pain and never ride again. When similar circumstances arise again, the same emotions come up and feed the fear, the anger, the shame, the guilt, the vulnerability we felt, and we become accustomed to feeling this way.

Thus, when we hold on to negative emotions, we can be negative towards people who had nothing to do with upsetting us, and our energy can affect their energy, causing ripple effects throughout our and others' relationships. These negative emotions then fester inside you and cause mental, spiritual, and physical problems. As the saying goes, holding on to negativity is like drinking poison and hoping the other person will die. You do yourself no good by holding grudges; it is simple as that.

You can forgive. But how can you truly forgive another person or even yourself? Forgiveness doesn't erase the memory. Is forgiveness then a temporary thing we use to push our pains to the back burner? Many use it as a way to superficially release something without working through it fully.

We need to forgive ourselves first and foremost. Often, forgiveness has nothing to do with the person we perceive as at fault. Even if the hurt was severe, we can find ways to releasing the emotion and forgiving ourselves. If we've been through a simple argument, forgiveness may start with acknowledgement, which enables mutual respect. Each person's emotional attachment is different, so the process of forgiveness will also be different.

You can truly say that you have forgiven someone when you no longer feel the emotions you used to feel—that is, when you feel neutral about the issue. It can take some time to reach this point depending on the degree of our attachment to the emotions. You can do many things to help this process along, but here is one exercise:

Make a list of the people you feel have hurt you and what happened, and then list why you feel the way you do about it. This list will help you see how you feel about each issue and why you feel it is an issue in the first place. Now, try to understand the other person's motives. Was the problem that caused the pain real, or did you imagine it? Did the other person hurt you deliberately, or was it an accident? You may find many motives you hadn't seen before. Next, ask yourself if you contributed to the problem in some way, and take responsibility for it. Ask yourself if this was karma for something you did in the past. By looking at the reasons behind a problem in this way, we can often see it differently, as the more aware we become, the more our perceptions change.

Instead of feeling sorry for yourself, feel sorry for the person who hurt you by saying to yourself, "If she knew how badly she affected me, she wouldn't have done that." Feel sorry that the other person is putting out bad karma, as it will eventually come back to bite them, and you are not in control of karma. Realize that what others do is only a reflection of what is inside them and has little to do with you. The person who wronged you may have been subjected to many bad things and simply didn't know how to act any better. It's impossible to completely know why people are the way they are, as we don't walk in their shoes.

Learn from what happened, and be grateful for this lesson. Showing gratitude can be hard, so start simple. Every morning when you wake up, list what you're grateful for. Start with the easy ones: the sleep you just had, a wonderful breakfast, the partner next to you, the sunshine. Then, move on to tougher points, the ones that seem negative when you first list them: the argument you had last night, the guy who cut you off while driving, the whinging child. Last, move on to the really tough ones: the child you lost, the partner who cheated, the boss who treated you poorly, the father who hit you or hurt others you love. When you can have gratitude for all those nasties in your life, forgiveness comes naturally.

The willingness to forgive is a sign of spiritual and emotional maturity. It is one of the great virtues to which we all should aspire. Imagine a world filled with individuals willing both to apologize and to accept apologies. Is there any problem that could not be solved by people who possess the humility and largesse to do these actions?

Notice that our attachments are about ourselves, not others, despite what we may think. Attributing problems to others is called *externalizing*. Every experience is about ourselves. The greater you choose to be, the greater the gift. Be understanding, not judgemental, of others' behaviour. Desire peace and harmony. Realize that there is no point in dwelling on the past. I agree that a victim or someone close to a victim of a crime can have difficulty forgiving the perpetrator, but learn, as I have, to look objectively at all situations, as doing so allows you to find compassion and ultimately love for others. Objectivity has allowed me to understand that other people's pains are not mine. This is not to say another's wrong actions were okay; it only means that I see the pain that led to those actions. We cross another person's path for a reason, although we won't see that reason until we're ready.

Feel that you have a great strength within, and embrace all of who you are without holding on to pains from the past.

Forgiveness is a lesson we must all learn in our own way. When we forgive, we release ourselves from the poison of hate, fear, and anger. We feel lighter, happier, and healthier. When you look deep within yourself with total honesty and come to the understanding that the only person being hurt by hanging on to a grudge is you, you can forgive yourself for your negative feelings, and then can forgive those who have hurt you, not for them but for yourself. You are then free to move forward with a lighter spirit and heart.

To forgive, I start with acceptance that what has happened has happened and can't be changed. Then, I choose to let the pain go and move past it because I create my own reality. I accept those who hurt me as they are, and I refuse to give my power to choose how I feel away to anyone. Learn from what happened. Take your wisdom with you and give the rest to God, the universe, or whatever power you believe in.

Attitude

Attitude plays a major role in our lives. Many people seem not to realize just how important their attitudes are. With the right attitude, we can accomplish anything, yet with a negative attitude, we might not even try. The universal law of attraction shows us that when we put out positive energy, we attract positivity into our lives, but if we put out negative energy, we attract negativity into our lives. Everything has both positive and negative elements and can be viewed from either side. You should look at the whole in any situation and be mindful of your thoughts in the moment. When we recognize the negative side and let it go, we can then focus on the positive and create a better life for ourselves and for each other.

Holding mostly a positive attitude can transform your life by bringing you much more happiness. Spending your time with other positive people adds to this happiness and helps you to notice others' negativity and choose to not let it affect you. By reinforcing a positive attitude, you will soon create even more positivity in your life.

We hold different attitudes towards different parts of our lives, including our work, friends, family, the places we go, and the things we encounter. By noticing these attitudes and asking ourselves whether each one is helping or hindering us, then we are better able to choose an attitude that will empower us in each part of life.

Many times our attitudes have become habits, and it can take time to change those habits. Our attitude also depends on our feelings, such as if we feel tired and sick or energetic and healthy, and on outside influences if we allow them to, as we can always choose how we let things outside ourselves affect us by focusing on the positive or on the negative.

When you spend a lot of time doing nothing, you feel less like doing anything—your attitude towards activity is negative. Yet when you are busy and have a positive attitude, then nothing seems like a problem. The old saying is true: "The more you do, the more you can do, and the less you do, the less you can do."

If you're tired and don't feel like doing anything, you can choose to do nothing and continue to feel tired and lazy and get nothing done, or you can choose to get up and do something and get the task done. You may still feel tired, but you likely will also feel proud that you accomplished something, and this may inspire you to do more. Eventually, you will likely feel better and more appreciative of being active, and your attitude has changed. There will always be times when we have a negative attitude, but when we make an effort to focus on the positive, then we'll have a positive attitude more often.

The following story, whose author is unknown, comes from Facebook, the story appeared in my newsfeed from a page I had liked and I have seen it a few times since. It relates to choosing your attitude and, therefore, whether you allow events in your life to affect you:

Grandmother Says: Carrots, Eggs, or Coffee, Which Are You?

A young woman went to her grandmother to tell her that her life was so hard that she didn't know how she was going to make it. She was so tired of fighting and struggling, as it seemed that when one problem was solved, a new one arose. She wanted to give up.

Her grandmother took her to the kitchen and filled three pots with water. She placed carrots in the first, eggs in the second, and ground coffee beans in the last. She let them sit and boil without saying a word.

After about ten minutes, she turned off the burners. She fished the carrots out and placed them in a bowl, pulled the eggs out and placed them in another bowl, and ladled the coffee into a third bowl. She then turned to her granddaughter and asked, "Tell me, what do you see?"

"Carrots, eggs, and coffee," replied the granddaughter.

The grandmother brought the young woman closer and asked her to feel the carrots. The young woman noted that they were soft. The grandmother then asked her to take an egg and break it. After pulling off the shell, she observed that the egg was hard-boiled. Finally, the grandmother asked the young woman to sip the coffee. The young woman smiled, as she tasted the rich flavour, and then she asked, "What's the point, Grandmother?"

The grandmother explained that each of these objects had faced the same adversity—boiling water—but each reacted differently.

The carrot went in strong and hard. However, in the boiling water, it had softened and became weak. The egg had been fragile; its thin outer shell had protected its liquid interior. But after sitting in the boiling water, its inside became hardened. The coffee beans were unique. When they sat in the boiling water, they changed the water.

"Which are you?" the grandmother asked. "When adversity knocks on your door, how do you respond? Are you a carrot, an egg, or coffee?"

Which are you?

Are you the carrot that seems strong but becomes soft during times of pain and adversity?

Are you the egg that starts with a soft heart but hardens with the heat? Did you have a fluid spirit but harden after a death, a break-up, a financial hardship, or some other trial, although your shell looks the same?

Or are you the coffee bean, which changes the hot water, the very circumstance that brings the pain? When the water gets hot, coffee releases its fragrance and flavour. If you are like the bean, when things are at their worst, do you get better and change the situation around you? At your darkest hour and during your greatest trial, do you elevate the world to another level?

Love

At times I ask myself, what is love? I see a lot of people place conditions and rules on their giving and receiving of love, but I see love itself as being unconditional. My understanding is that love is a powerful, even overwhelming emotion that triggers feelings of joy and bliss. Giving and receiving love makes us feel happy and content. There are many types of love, which each differ in intensity. The love you feel for your parents and siblings, your children, your partner, your extended relations, your friends, and strangers, and there is also the love you feel for pets and other animals, places, and things. You can love special foods, special occasions, and special events. Even though the love you feel for each of these differs, it is all love. Whether it is given or received, I see love as one thing: a whole, pure, positive energy that is unconditional, unjudging, strong, beautiful, healing, and enriching in many ways. It is why we choose to spend time with certain people, to listen to certain people, to allow certain people to influence us, to tolerate certain people, and to sacrifice for certain people. It is possible to be angry with someone yet still love him or her.

Sometimes those we love don't treat us with respect, compassion, and consideration, and it may be best to distance ourselves from them for a while or even forever. If you decide to do this, realize you do this not because you put conditions on the love you give but because you're doing what's best for you, as the most important love is the love for yourself. You deserve to be treated with respect, and this includes self-respect. Love unconditionally, and give love and accept the love you are given equally.

I love with all that I am, and I love all that is, for I am connected to everything. Everything is part of me. I am love! I live for love and I would die for love. Love is the most important thing to give and receive!

Relationships

We engage in many different types of relationships in our lives, including those with family, friends, colleagues, and lovers. We can choose some of these relationships but not others. You don't choose who you are related to, for the most part, we don't get to choose who we work with. We do choose our friends, our partners, and our lovers.

You are connected to family members by blood, but more than this, you are connected to them emotionally and spiritually. Whether you see family members often or every now and then, you will always share a bond with them that is unlike any other bonds. When we disagree with family members, the bond we share often overrides the dispute and allows us to more easily forgive and forget and continue with the relationship, but this is not always the case. The love I have for my children and my mother is unconditional, so we may disagree, but this does not change my love for them, and I will always forgive them. In other families, when members have had disagreements, they have totally ended their relationship. We each have our reasons for choosing to feel how we feel about other people, regardless of the bonds we share with them. Often many factors lead family members to sever their ties, and they have to do what they feel is right and what is in their own best interests, regardless of the love they feel or bonds they share.

At work, we will often find that we get on with our co-workers because we have similar interests that led us to our jobs or that have nothing to do with work, and we can form great friendships with these co-workers. However, we may not get on well with colleagues for any number of reasons. We face many pressures to get the work done effectively and efficiently and to meet deadlines or quotas, and these pressures affect people differently. We also face power disparities, with those in positions of authority over other staff members. Some people are well suited to positions of power and maintain a happy work environment, while others abuse any power they are given and make the work environment miserable. When we work in a happy environment, we can enjoy going to work and being with our co-workers, but when we work in an environment where we feel we are not respected, where we are put down by others, or where we are made to feel bad in some other way, we'll feel negative about our work. We can decide to put up with such treatment or to do something about it, including seeking employment elsewhere. Often it is our own attitude towards work and towards those we work with that determines whether we have beneficial work relationships.

When we form those relationships that we choose, we attract or are attracted to people who put out energies similar to our own. We may have similar interests or tastes, and we build these relationships over time by spending time together and nurturing these commonalities. Whether with friends or our partners, we tolerate some things because of the good we get from the relationship. However, there is a limit to what we will tolerate, regardless of the type of relationship. If we find ourselves putting ourselves out for another to the point that we give more than we receive from the relationship, then we will often end the relationship. If we change the energy that we put out or another person changes his or her energy, we may just drift apart.

I think that relationships are a lot like a bank account. Each person makes deposits into the relationship or withdrawals from the relationship. When we show respect, have compassion, show understanding, give compliments, have fun, give encouragement, trust, love, or otherwise show appreciation for the other person and the relationship, we deposit positive energy into the relationship, and if both members continue to make such deposits, the balance will increase and remain healthy.

But we can also make withdrawals from our relationship account. When one person takes without giving, he or she makes a withdrawal from the account. If he or she shows disrespect, or puts you down, argues, or makes you feel that he or she doesn't care for you or doesn't value you or uses you, they make withdrawals. If the relationship drains you, then there are more withdrawals being made from the relationship than deposits, then the balance falls into the red, and you may decide that it's best to close the account and end that particular relationship.

Every relationship has such an account. If you want your relationships to grow and be healthy, then you need to make more deposits than you do withdrawals.

I have had many friendships over the years, and many of these have simply faded away simply because the energies we put out changed or we found other interests and just stopped seeing each other. I still like these people, and in each case, neither person did anything to upset the other enough to end the relationship. In some cases, friends are guided into our lives to help us or for us to help them or both before we drift apart.

Worry, Anxiety, Stress, and Depression

For much of my life, I have suffered from low self-esteem, depression, anxiety, and high stress. I worried about many things constantly. I was not happy with areas of my life. I complained about this and whinged about that, I blamed others for my problems, and I really let life affect me in a negative way. Even if nothing was wrong, I worried and stressed about what might go wrong. It wasn't easy to change myself from here, as my mind was set in the habit of negative thinking.

I created my own anxiety and stress, as they don't depend on conditions outside of us. It is not a happy life to always deal with these emotions, and they caused many problems throughout my life. Worry and anxiety led to stress, which caused problems in my mind and body. I felt tired and suffered frequent headaches, which led to more worry and stress, which ended up as depression. I often didn't know why I was depressed, and although I didn't like feeling this way, I felt helpless to change.

I seriously considered ending it all many times, but thankfully, something always stopped me, so I struggled on with these emotions.

I underwent many treatments to help me cope with these feelings. Doctors gave me antidepressants, which helped temporarily but had side effects. The body can develop a tolerance to the beneficial effects of many of this type of medication, so they become unhelpful but still cause the side effects. Many are also difficult to stop taking, as the body undergoes withdrawal. I have had to change medication a few times because of the side effects or they no longer worked for me. Antidepressants can help relieve suffering, but they are not a solution to the problem.

I also saw many counsellors and therapists and talked about my thoughts and feelings, and some of these professionals were quite good. I found it beneficial to talk about my thoughts with another person in order to get another perspective and to just release them instead of keeping the issue bottled up. Counsellors and therapists advised me on techniques to help me to cope with my life, and this did help, but my habit of negative thinking kicked back in when I was on my own, and the struggle with those dominant thoughts continued. I've searched for the solution to my anxiety and depression for many years, and to be honest, there isn't a quick way to permanently solve them.

We all suffer from anxiety and depression, we all worry, and we all deal with stress. These are all natural. When we're balanced, these aren't big problems for us to handle. However, our minds can blow them out of proportion, influenced by our upbringing and our experiences. If your parents didn't know how to control these emotions well, then chances are you were never taught how to control your own emotions So how do you learn to deal with anxiety, stress, and depression? How can you get out of patterns of negative thinking so they no longer affect your life negatively?

The solution was simple but very hard to do, and it took time.! No one else could do it for me, but I didn't have to do it by myself. I found it helpful to learn about my conditions by reading up on the causes and effects of anxiety and depression and techniques I could use to help me cope with them. I looked into what triggered these feelings and what started me down the road in the first place. Besides medication from doctors, working with nutritionists and naturopaths to sort out your diet can help, as what you eat can influence your emotions. In the end, I needed to stop focusing on the negative thoughts.

The more you focus on what you don't want in your life, the more you attract these conditions to you. Therefore, you need to change your thinking to change your life. To do this, you need to pay attention to your thoughts and take control of the power of your mind. Meditation is a useful tool to sharpen the mind and be more observant of its patterns if it's practised regularly. Reading positive affirmations and self-help books and listening to motivational CDs and podcasts can also help.

You can train yourself to avoid negative self-talk. If you tell yourself, "I don't let my emotions control me!" your mind will focus on the negative tone in this simple sentence. "I let my emotions control me." However, if you leave out the problem from the sentence completely and change the statement to something positive, like "I am in control of my emotions," you will focus on the positive. If you always pay attention to these little patterns and change them by leaving out the words that relate to the problem, you can focus on the positive. Also surround yourself with positive, happy people who will support you and comfort you, as they will also help you look for the positives.

My husband has been my saviour over the past eight years. I give him a lot of credit for helping me and putting up with me. He always talks positively, and he always points out when I am not positive. Whenever I feel depressed or anxious, I talk to him about my feelings, and he helps me see the situation differently. I always

Suzie Price

feel better afterwards. Having someone like this in your life can make a huge difference in changing your thought patterns.

As you become more aware of your thoughts, when you notice yourself thinking negatively, you can stop yourself and shift your focus to the opposite of the negative thought. If you feel depressed, then look for the positive side of what caused you to feel this way or focus on something that makes you feel happy and distracts you from those negative thoughts. If you feel anxious, then focus on being confident, and think about all of the things that could go right instead of the things that may go wrong. Look for the things you like instead of focusing on what you don't like. Adjust your attitude and try not to judge, and let go of others' judgement. What someone else thinks about you is none of your business and doesn't matter to you. All that matters is what you think or feel, and you can always choose that. Only you can make you happy, sad, angry, excited, or anything else. You decide how you let things affect you!

It took me many years to get my mind to where it is today. I still get anxious and feel depressed at times, but these times are fewer and farther between, and the intensity of these negative emotions is much less severe, so I can shake these feelings off much more easily. I suffer from fewer stress headaches, too, those I do have last for shorter periods and are less intense. When I look back, I can see that I've come far and have changed markedly. I didn't notice the changes at first, but as time passed, the difference I saw within myself was amazing. I also really notice how negatively many other people talk about themselves, their lives, their friends, and everything else.

My life has improved so much over the past eight years, and I feel these positive changes in both my inner world and my outer life because I have become a more positive person. Even when you take little steps, you are still moving forward, and if you don't like where you are, doing something is better than staying put.

Being Spiritual

Being spiritual means for me that I respect myself, other people, and all life. I treat myself and others with respect and without critical judgement. I understand that all people have their own beliefs, opinions, and paths, and just because we're on different paths doesn't mean we won't end up in the same place. I try to love my fellow humans regardless of their race, religion, point of view, or way of life. I practice tolerance and forgive. I always try to speak kind words with a kind heart from a place of love. I try to see others as equals and love all equally. I share what I have with others without expectations, as I see giving as its own reward.

I understand that everything is both positive and negative, and what we perceive depends on our focus, so I try to focus on the positive. I treat others with respect and show compassion and understanding towards all life. I am open with my views, but I know that I don't know everything and am always learning. I try to remain centred within myself. I also try to always be honest and to be the best that I can be in whatever I do.

I believe in God/Goddess, although my perception of God may be different to others'. I believe in angels and spirits, and I believe we are all connected as part of the same energy, so it is possible to communicate with any other living thing, including animals, plants, and even the planet itself. I believe that this is true not just on our planet but in the entire universe.

I do not believe in hell or the devil. I accept that there is good and bad, right and wrong in everything. If I choose to perceive something as good or bad, right or wrong, positive or negative, then that is my choice, and it doesn't mean that the thing is only what I perceive it to be, as another's perception will be different. I believe the only hell and evil are those that we create for ourselves through the choices we make and the way we treat each other. We all choose whether our lives are hell or heaven. Make your choices and create your reality.

God and Heaven

I believe that God is part of everything, including me, and is connected to all things. Scientific evidence tells us that our bodies are made up of stardust, as all of the elements in our bodies except hydrogen and helium were created in stars. This is true of all matter. I also know that all things are also energy vibrating at different rates, and I see God as the source of that energy. This is energy connected to all things, both those that we are able to detect and those that we are not yet capable of detecting. Therefore, it seems reasonable to me to perceive God as the source energy of all things in the universe. I also see God as a dual entity, or both male and female, as both God and Goddess.

I see everything in the universe, including us, as energy, and our soul as the seat of our life energy. When this energy is in human form, it contains mass and vibrates more slowly, or at a lower frequency, than when it is released from our human form.

When we pass from our human form, the soul is released from the body and joins other energies that vibrate at this higher frequency. It retains all the memories from the life it just left and the memories from all its previous lives. It is able to connect to a range of vibrations, including those energies still vibrating at the lower frequency of the human form.

In our human form, most of us are only capable of seeing and hearing energies with a small range of frequencies and wavelengths. In fact, the visible light that our eyes can see makes up less than 1 per cent of the electromagnetic light spectrum, and the audible sound that our ears can hear makes up less than 1 per cent of the electromagnetic acoustic spectrum. With the aid of technology, we are able to see and hear much more of these spectra, but there is still much that we cannot see and cannot hear. The abilities I have as a medium allow me to tune into the otherwise imperceptible parts of these spectra, so I am able to see and hear things that most other people can't, including passed souls.

All people can tune into other frequencies in this way, but some people do so more easily than others, and we often get mixed signals or poor reception.

Spirits have told me that they can see us and hear us, they can still connect to us in many other ways. They watch us and try to help us. They remain with us; they simply vibrate at a frequency that is beyond the range of the average human's energy. Almost all of the spirits I've connected to have been happy, and I've felt their love and positive energy, their peace and freedom. Rarely have I come across spirits that made me feel uncomfortable or scared, and I believe this is simply because of my own energy is positive and loving which attracts similar energies.

I believe that heaven isn't so much a place or a dimension as it is a state of being, a state of bliss, contentment, understanding, acceptance, peace and love. Our spirits can easily vibrate at the frequency of this state, but it is possible to attain this state of being while we are alive. You can find heaven on earth, here and now, by living positively, lovingly, respectfully, honestly, kindly, and with tolerance, understanding, and forgiveness for others, the environment, and yourself, and by recognizing that others are part of who you are.

Death and the Continuation of the Soul

There are many different beliefs about what happens to us when we die. Some people believe that death is the end, that there is nothing afterwards. These people do not believe in an eternal soul or spirit. Many other people believe that we do have a soul or spirit and have devised many theories about what happens to this part of us when we pass on from this life. Some believe that we are reborn, or reincarnated, and that we could come back as another person or as an animal or another type of living being.

Many belief systems say that the choices we make in this life will determine where we will spend eternity or how we will be reborn. If people are bad, they will spend eternity in hell or will come back as an insect or other undesirable life form as punishment for their sins. If people are good and live by the religion's rules, they will go to a magical place called heaven or will come back to live a happier life.

We all have free will and so are able to choose for ourselves what we want to believe. However, many people try to force their beliefs onto others, and adults teach their children the belief systems of their cultures, and it can then be difficult for those children to change their beliefs as they grow. Whatever you choose to believe is up to you; only you can decide what is right or wrong for you.

My observations of how the world works, tell me that everything works in cycles. When night falls, I know the sun will return in a few hours to my side of the world again. When summer ends, I know that it will return in nine months, as it is part of the cycle of seasons. Life, too, is a cycle. Matter comes from energy and eventually returns to energy. Therefore, this makes reincarnation a possibility. The question that we need to answer I suppose is how, exactly, the process works.

I believe that the energy within us seeks an ultimate state of being, full enlightenment, if you will. What that all really boils down to is that as each soul learns lessons, its vibrations are raised to a purer form. We're here on earth to learn these lessons. If we fail to learn a lesson, we get to try all over again, but if we succeed, we move on to the next lesson until we have reached the ultimate state. At this time, I suspect we move on to another plane of existence, where we most certainly get a whole new set of lessons to learn, and thus the cycle continues. In the readings I've done over the years, animals have often come through in spirit; however, I couldn't say if a human could come back as an animal or vice versa, as spirit hasn't given me this message. However, many cultures do believe this happens.

I therefore see death as a transformation and not an end. When our souls leave our bodies, we remain aware of what is happening around us. We are greeted by other spirits with whom we have a connection, such as close family members or friends who passed before us. Angels, or pure beings of love and light, guide us through this transition. They show us a review of our lives that includes the good and bad choices we made that affected ourselves and others. We then go to a level on the spiritual plane depending on our choices where celestial beings teach and guide us and other spirits. Most souls need to work through a number of spiritual levels before they are able to move on. As spirits, we are able to move between these levels as we need to.

Spirits often tell me that they can smoke or drink and sing and dance—whatever they enjoyed in life—as much as they like now and are having a party with their family members in spirit. They always say that they're having a great time. I don't think that spirits can literally do all the things they enjoyed while they were alive; instead, I believe they're expressing to their loved ones that they are happy, free, and at peace.

As spirits, we are able to visit our loved ones here on this plane of existence at any time, and we watch over them and help them and the guides who are with them.

In spirit, we feel less emotional and more detached, as there is no judgement, no right or wrong, no good and bad. There is no jealousy or spite or resentment or hate. There is positive and negative, light and dark, understanding, compassion, love, and peace. Things simply are what they are. Everything is connected, and we can connect to anything at any time.

Once we have progressed through our lessons and most of our connections from our human existence have faded or joined us in spirit, we can choose to be reborn in human form and continue our journey through existence. We can choose who we come back as and our parents and other family members, and we see what the blueprint of our lives' events, including our death which I believe is pre-determined.

People often complain about others and are even glad when they die. If someone has committed murder or caused a lot of suffering for a lot of people, then it can be easy to think that they deserve to die. Call me crazy, but I know that only angels and other spirits truly rejoice when someone passes on from this existence, as they welcome home the soul of the departed. The spirit within my mortal body sends them love. When someone has lost his or her way and lived without love, compassion, and respect for all beings that inhabit our planet, I feel sad for his or her soul, for I know it will have to endure much hardship. Whether criminals or children, whether I or others have felt wronged by them, I forgive and love all as I would my own child, for we are all one in the eyes of the creator.

Angels and Spirits

Millions of people throughout history have claimed to see spirits and angels appear before them. Many of these people, like myself, also claim to be able to communicate with these beings. Those who have not experienced such a phenomenon can find these claims hard to believe, yet people still make them. I cannot convince you that these claims are true, as you must draw your own conclusions. However, I will relate my own experiences with these beings, as they are true for me.

I have had many experiences with what I believe to be spirits and angels. The first experience occurred when I had my accident, and since then such encounters have become a normal part of my life. I don't know why everybody can't see spirits and angels as I can, and I have often wondered why this is so. I can only assume it is because we all have different abilities. Some people are good at working with their hands, others are good at thinking and inventing and science, and I'm good at communicating with the spirit world. We are all wired differently for different reasons and purposes. I believe we all are capable of communicating with spirit; but for some people it is easy and for others it is hard.

Some photographs of angels and spirits, especially pictures of orbs, have been developed, and many of them have been exposed as fraudulent alterations, and many people assume others are also fraudulent. Scientists who have examined these pictures have found evidence of natural phenomena that explains the appearance of these images that look like angels, spirits, or orbs. I can accept that most of these pictures are just fake and explanations for the images can be found; however, when you consider that the human eye can see less than 1 per cent of the electromagnetic spectrum, you realize that there is much more in the universe than what we can see. Science has developed greatly over the past two centuries, and with the aid of scientific equipment, we are able to detect much more of the electromagnetic spectrum than ever before, but there is still much that is undetectable. Consider this: Rainbows exist to us because we have conical photoreceptors in our eyes that can detect the colours; to animals without cones, rainbows do not exist. So you don't just look at a rainbow, your sensory organs create it. Pretty amazing! Because of these ideas, I choose to remain open to the possibility that some pictures of angels, spirits, and orbs are real.

The following sections describe what angels and spirits are and why they are here.

Angels

Angels are pure-energy beings. Their energy vibrates at a very high frequency, and they are closely connected to the source energy, God. Many people believe that angels have never walked on earth in human form, whereas others believe that angels have at some stage been able to take human form and that they are evolved from spirit. That is, as a spirit or soul grows, it vibrates at increasingly higher frequencies, and eventually, after many lives in many forms, a soul reaches the very high vibration of an angel. I don't know which is true. I believe that there are many different types of angels based on their level of ascension, each of which is associated with a different task:

- Guardian angels watch over each living person. Your angel holds the blueprint for your life and guides you to follow it and guides the other angels and spirits who are assigned to you. It's this angel's job to protect you and help you throughout your life.
- Specialist angels perform many specific tasks. Some are healers who assist you when you're unwell, some are warriors who give you courage and strength, some are teachers. These angels have many more roles, too, to help you with whatever you need.
- Guidance angels guide our souls when we die, taking our souls through our life reviews and guides the soul where to go. Some of them assist those who grieve for the soul that has passed on.
- Archangels are highly evolved and play a major role in all realms. They guide the flow of existence and the process of evolution of the soul. Each archangel specializes in different areas.

Spirits

Spirits are our souls in energy form. I believe that every life form, human, plant, animal, the land, and all energy forms contain a life force, or spirit, and when they cease to live, that is returned to its original state, where it continues to learn and grow and, thus, raise its vibration before transforming again into a physical body.

This process takes some time, during which the spirit retains consciousness and the memories of all of our experiences from all its forms since the beginning of its existence. At this time, it is also more able to connect with the source energy and all other energy forms than it is during our lives. Our spirits are self-aware and omni-aware, or aware of everything that is happening, all at the same time. Therefore, they can know what is happening to everyone they have ever been connected to at any given moment.

As spirits are energy beings, they exist in a dimension that is not accessible to most people in our dimension, or a state of being that exists within the place where we are. We living human beings have limited abilities to perceive what is around us, but some of us can connect to this dimension where we are from and where we are going. I am able to glimpse into what the eye cannot see and hear what the ear cannot hear by connecting with our source energy and tuning into the right frequencies. Spirits and other beings of energy are able to create subtle changes in our dimension as well, tuning themselves to a frequency that allows them to be seen, heard, or felt: they can move solid objects, turn devices on and off, and communicate with us through dreams and thoughts.

Spirit Guides

I have many spirit guides. Some have been with me since childhood, and hundreds more have come to me when it was their time to help me. Everyone has spirit guides, and they guide us throughout our lives. I am able to hear my guides speaking to me through all of my psychic senses. I recognize each one by the feeling of its energy, not its name. Names are not important to spirit guides, and they often keep their real names secret, giving you a name that you can relate to so that you have a tag with which to identify a vibration. The number of guides we have at any given time varies depending on our needs and on our openness to listen for their insights. Spirit guides can give you warnings, they can show you the future and the past, and they can help you healing and find emotional balance. I talk with my guides every day; I ask them questions, and they give me answers. When you learn to trust in your guides, you can truly benefit from their presence.

Many people have asked me how they can communicate with their spirit guides. This is really quite simple, but it does take faith, trust, awareness, sensitivity, openness, willingness, and practice. First, you have to be open to the communication, believing that they are there and that you can communicate with them. You then have to let go of your expectations for how the communication will take place. Often the communication between you and your guides is very subtle, not like talking to another person. Messages can come in any form, so you will need to be aware and use all your senses to receive these messages. Next, tell your guides that you are ready, willing, and open to communicate with them, and ask them to connect with you. Trust that you are capable of communicating with them, and trust in the information you receive.

I recommend practicing meditation to build your awareness and sensitivity and to call on your spirit guides. I also recommend that you learn about how your psychic senses work and practice using them.

When you communicate with any spirits, whether they be your guides, your departed loved ones, or angels, you use your mind. Many people wonder if such a communication is just their imagination at work and doubt what they picked up on. This is always the biggest obstacle to this type of communication. I remind people that there are no such thing as coincidences, that everything happens for a reason and in perfect synchronicity, so if something in your head is real for you, then it doesn't matter if it is not real for others.

Fate

I believe, as many others believe, that our fate is written before we are born. We can see what will happen in our lives, who our parents will be, and what our names will be, all before we are conceived, and we choose the lives we will live. Our deaths are also planned. When you look at your palm, you can see a blueprint of this life in the lines and the shape that you see. I can tell a lot about a person from reading the lines on the hand, the shape of the hand, and other detail of it. Because I'm also psychic, I can tell people the past, present, and future events of their lives. Because of this evidence, I have no doubt that many of the events of our lives are preordained. Fate is a given, and we will all fulfil our own fates, but destiny is another matter.

Fate is what is written into the blueprint of your life, and it usually can't be altered, yet we create our own destinies, and can change them, by our choices and our attitudes and thoughts, as the attitudes and thoughts we allow to occupy our minds attract more of the same to us.

Another way to look at it is that fate determines major life events, such as whether you'll have children, who your partners will be, and when you will die. Destiny, on the other hand, relates to our smaller life choices that affect our health, our finances, and our general attitudes. Fate determines what will happen, and destiny determines how it will happen.

There is some speculation about whether fate can be altered, and I personally believe that nothing is set in stone. Therefore, fate is somewhat flexible. However, if something is meant to happen, it will eventually find a way to happen. I also believe we each have a guardian angel who knows our fate, and it is this angel's job to guide us to where we are meant to be. Other angels and spirits assist this guardian angel, and these energies play a major role in shaping our lives.

Psychic Protection

Psychic protection is an awareness of the energies around you and the ability to choose which energies you want to allow into your own energy field and which ones to keep out. There are many ways to protect yourself and many reasons why you should protect yourself. As an energy being, you continually give off energy and absorb energy. Psychic protection can keep you from absorbing the wrong energy. Not all of the energies you absorb are good for you. Some can be quite draining, leaving you feeling flat or agitated or angry or depressed, while others can lift you up and make you feel good.

If you're in a room with other people, and new people who are yelling and are aggressive come in, the energy of the room and people with you changes. Likewise, your energy changes if you see someone crying or if those around you are laughing and having fun. You can feel and recognize many types of energy, but there are other energies that you may not notice at all.

Many have reported feeling negative spirits attached to them or to places. This spiritual attachment comes in many forms. I have helped some people who have suffered from this type of attachment, which can lead to ill physical and mental health for the victim.

Just as you can control the energy you put out into the universe, you can also control which energies you allow to come into your space. Many of us do this instinctively. When we're around positive energy, our energy fields open, and when we're threatened by negative energy, then they close to protect us. We can also get into bad habits that prevent this from happening.

To filter the energy you let in, first, observe the energies around you. If you notice something that you do not want to take on, then move to a place where the energy is different. If this is not possible, then some of the negative energy may attach to you unless you use a protection method. You can learn a lot about this through meditation, but to list a few, you can:

- Call on your angels for help. Simply ask for help aloud or in your mind, and they will be there.
- Imagine yourself inside a pink or white bubble, wearing a protective cloak, or carrying a shield that fends off the energy, reflecting it back to its source. Any mental image of a barrier like this, even a rose bush with thorns, that blocks the negative energy will do.
- Tell your subconscious mind to block out all negative energy and to allow only positive energy into your space. Do this by paying attention to what you are taking in. Have total faith in your ability to protect yourself.
- Wear talismans or jewellery with protective qualities or symbols on them.
- Carry or wear obsidian, clear or smoky quartz, or other protective crystals.
- Cast a spell or say a chant.

- Spray flower essences or burn herbs to neutralize negative electromagnetic energy.
- Colours can be used to protect you as well, wearing pink or blue can repel negativity.
- Invisible light or call in pure light to surround and protect you.
- Acoustic Vibrations can also be used; Play drums, bells, chimes, crystal bowls, or clap or chant to send out protective acoustic vibrations.

You can search the internet or look for books with information on psychic protection to find more methods to use, and choose something that feels comfortable for you. As a general rule, keep it simple so that you can easily use the technique you choose when you need to.

When negative energy is attached to you or to a place such as your home, there are also a number of ways to clear away this energy. Burning white sage or other types of smudge sticks will lift negative energy and lighten the energy around in a room. This can be combined with the use of playing bells, and prayer or instructions, telling the energy to go, and praying for help in removing it. Keep your mind focused on removing the energy, and send it love and pure energy to raise its vibration to allow it to move.

Spells and prayers have been written for this purpose, so you can search for or ask others to teach you many ones that will work for your particular problem.

Remember that energies vibrating at or near the same frequency are attracted to each other, so if you put out positive energy, you will attract this energy to you and repel energies at lower frequencies.

Portals and Dimensions

People believe that certain places hold unique energy and power and are portals to other dimensions. Others doubt the existence of such places. I believe that what people call other dimensions are all part of this place where we are; we just can't detect or connect to them, as they are different levels of vibrational energy.

There is no doubt in my mind that places can and do hold energy. Some places feel light and positive, and others feel heavy and negative. Places where a lot of negative things happened hold negative energy, and you can feel the heavy vibrations there. This might be the case in gaols, asylums, the sites of murders, or even in homes where many fights took place. If you absorb this negative energy, then it can change your energy, making you feel drained, irritable, angry, and it can even cause headaches or other sicknesses. Likewise, places can hold positive energy. These might be sacred sites, churches, homes that are full of love, or other places where positive things happened. These places feel nice and make a visitor feel happy, peaceful, calm, and uplifted, even after you leave.

Knowing this, it stands to reason that there are places where the energy is so light and positive or so heavy and negative that their vibrations can raise or lower a visitor's vibration to such a frequency that it is easier for him or her to connect to other dimensions, or vibrational energies. Many such places exist on our planet, and for those who are in tune with their own vibrational energies, these places can hold great power.

I also believe that portals can be manipulated using incantations and symbols. A lady once asked me to come to her home, as one of her rooms was always very cold and had a horrible feeling to it. It had been her son's bedroom, but he would sleep in the lounge room instead, and he became withdrawn and agitated. The lady told me that she had been friends with a witch but that they had fallen out, so the lady thought that the witch had placed a spell on her home.

I asked a Wiccan priestess who is a good friend of mine to help me cleanse this home. When we arrived, the lady welcomed us in and took us into the bedroom. The room was very cold, and I could see what looked like a portal in the middle of the room and half-animal, half-human creatures. No one else could see these but me, and I felt very uncomfortable. The priestess and I cleansed the room and the rest of the house, and the priestess said an incantation to close the portal. After we had finished, the room felt normal and was no longer cold. The lady sent me a couple of messages afterwards to thank me, saying that her family noticed the difference in the home straight away and that her son was back to his old self. This experience definitely opened my mind to the possibility that portals exist.

Living Your Life's Purpose

Many people wonder about the purpose of life, about what they're meant to do and what they're doing wrong. Many people find this question hard to answer, and many believe that there is no answer. I have found the answer to this question, so I see this as a very simple matter. Each person must find a purpose that feels true for him or her. I found the answer in awareness. I am a very sensitive person, and in my work as a medium, I need to be aware with all of my senses to tune into messages from spirit. I also meditate regularly in order to develop my abilities and become more aware and better able to notice little things and pay more attention to everything that is happening.

Through this awareness, I've noticed that when things happen easily and just flow, then they are meant to happen and you are on the right path and following your purpose. However, when obstacles block your path and progress is hard, when no matter what you do, things just don't seem to be happening, this is a clear indication you are going the wrong way. You may be doing something at the wrong time, you may be with the wrong person, or you may be working on the wrong project. At these times, you should reassess your direction. You may find that there is a different way, a better way, or a completely new direction, that you are not aware of.

For example, when I was with some men, I often ignored signs that this wasn't a relationship for me. Some relationships lasted longer than others, but they all had problem after problem. Yet when I met Stephen, things just flowed, and we still rarely encounter problems in our relationship. When I tried to push my singing career, I encountered problem after problem, roadblock after roadblock. I did have some success, but something always prevented me from getting where I wanted to go. Yet with my work as a psychic medium, things have just flowed. I have to pay attention and take advantage of opportunities when they appear, and take actions but these opportunities seem to fall into my lap, and I don't have to force progress in my career.

So, if you wonder what your life purpose is, then pay attention to what is happening in your life. Notice when your life flows easily and when you hit roadblocks. You may have more than one life purpose, so what you're doing today may be different to what you'll be doing in the future. It may be that you are meant to do this for now, but it may just be to teach you what you need to know for your next purpose. Roads are never straight for long. They have twists and turns, hills and valleys, and many places where you can turn off and head in a totally different direction. If you are following your purpose, then the drive will be easy; however, if you encounter roadblocks, look for turn-offs. You will be led in the direction you need to go. What is meant to be will always find a way to happen.

Karma

I am a big believer in karma, or the law of attraction—what you put out in thought and energy will come back to you. For example:

- o If you show respect to others, then they will show respect to you. If you show disrespect to others, then they will show disrespect to you.
- o If you show love and compassion to others, then others will show love and compassion to you. If you show anger and resentment to others, then others will show anger and resentment to you.
- o If you are honest and trust others, then others will be honest with you and will trust you. If you lie and express distrust, then other people will lie to you and won't trust you.
- o If you think positively and do positive things, then positive things will be attracted to you. If you think negatively and do negative things, then negative things will attract to you.

Keep in mind that what you give does not always come back directly. You may give respect to one person, but another person may return it. When you are honest with someone, and he or she may tell you lies, but in general, other people will be more honest with you. Remember that what others put out is their karma and is what they will receive, so don't concern yourself with what others do. Instead, focus on what you put out.

You get what you give, so choose what you give with this in mind, and realize that whatever is happening in your life now is a product of the energy that you have given out in the past. If you would like to improve your future, then pay attention to the energy you give out today.

I believe that karma has a lot more to do with your life now than your next life, except where your current actions might leave unresolved energy with whatever lesson you might be learning. The idea of past lives is connected to a belief in reincarnation. I do believe that our past lives echo down the corridors of time and that we can find their shadows in our current lives.

The Law of Attraction

The concept of karma—that you get back what you give out— is accepted in many societies. If you put out good vibes, you get good vibes back; if you put out negative vibes, you will get negative vibes back. Not only this, but whatever you put out is sent back to you three times more intensely. The law of attraction works on this principles, but there is more to it and it is much more important than you may have ever realized. It is a universal law of the energy of all things.

As we've discussed, your body gives out many different energies and absorbs other energies, and your subconscious mind controls and communicates with your energy and other energies. Your subconscious mind also brings to you what you want and need. It does this by sending out energy that vibrates at the same frequency as the thing that you want or need. Like attracts like. Birds of a feather flock together.

The bad news is that the subconscious mind does not distinguish between good and bad or right and wrong. It does not to sort out what you want or don't want; it simply sends out the energy of what you focus on and believe. The more you focus on something, the faster you attract it to you. When you add your emotions to your thoughts, you intensify the signal from your subconscious mind.

Most people don't focus on anything for long; our thoughts are often all over the place. We also don't take enough notice of what we think about. Many of us worry and stress, and by doing so, without realizing it, we attract more of what we worry and stress about. To overcome this, you need to take more control over your subconscious mind. This can be achieved through meditation and awareness of your thoughts. Meditation is like a magical key that can unlock a whole new world. It can benefit your life in many ways, so it is well worth taking a little time to add this practice to your daily routine.

Another problem comes from our beliefs. As we grow up and go through life, beliefs become conditioned in our minds. We believe things we see, experience, and are taught. We encounter problems when we work with the law of attraction if we try to attract something to us that we don't truly believe, as doing so sends our subconscious mind contradictory messages.

To attract something to us, we need to put it out there and truly believe that it will come to us. You need to trust, without a doubt, that this will work, as doubt will repel what you want, as it puts out the opposite energy to trust.

If you only put out that you desire something, the subconscious mind will send out the energy of desire and will bring back only more desire, not the actual thing that you desire. You therefore need to put out the energy of already having what we desire. For example, if you want to bring in money, you must first believe you have the money. Fake it until you make it. Train yourself to believe things that you know for a fact are not true yet. You can do this by using affirmations and vision boards and visualization meditations in which you see yourself as already having what you want.

Another key ingredient to the law of attraction is gratitude. Show gratitude for everything you already have and everything you are trying to attract as though you already have it. Gratitude will magnify the energy you put out and make it more positive.

The next step is to expect things to happen. As you put out energy for something, the universe will give you opportunities to have it. You'll be sent signs and chances to obtain what you want or to move closer to obtaining it. You need to look for opportunities, ideas, and people that come out of nowhere to help bring you what you are attracting. Pay attention to what appears, and use your intuition. You'll know if something feels right, and if it does, take action to get what you're attracting.

Sometimes you'll reach a goal out of the blue, but other times you'll need to work towards a goal over time requiring you to take actions to make it happen.

The subconscious mind is amazing. It operates our organs and retains memories. It also regulates the energy coming into and going out of our bodies, as we've just discussed. It also sets about getting you what your conscious mind focuses on. By controlling your conscious mind and training it to focus on what you really want, you use it to instruct your subconscious mind, and then you can have the things you want, do the things you like to do, and you will be much happier and your life more complete.

If you notice yourself thinking negatively, or about anything that you don't want in your life. Stop! This is so important. You have to learn to let go of negative thoughts and replace them with positive thoughts. The more you are able to do this, the quicker you will attract positive things into your life.

Whether you want to win a race, find love, have money, drive a new car, go on a holiday, get a job, or achieve any goal, the law of attraction will shape your life to bring it about if you put out the right energy.

If you go through life without using the law of attraction for your benefit, than you risk getting to a point where things constantly go wrong. The more you hold on to negative energy, the worse things will become. Holding negative things inside and burying them eventually manifests physical illnesses. Instead, always look for the good in even the very bad. Notice any negativity, and observe it but then let go of it. Forgive and *let go*! Be more positive and loving towards everything.

Now, determine what it is you want. Think about every area of your life. What do you want to change? How can you improve? What makes you happy? Ask these questions about your relationships, finances, health and fitness, personal possessions, holidays, and spirituality.

Many people have trouble imagining what they really want at first, so before you think about this too much, make a list of all the things you don't want in every area of your life. You will need lots of paper, a pen, and a bit of time. By doing this, you can acknowledge these things and let them go. By acknowledging them, you'll recognize them if they pop up in the future, and by letting them go, you choose not to give them any of your energy. This creates an empty space in your energy field for other stuff to fill. Now, turn your focus to what you do want. Don't be afraid to think big. You can create whatever it is you want. We are all co-creators with God. List each item, and write as much detail as you can about it. Be specific but flexible, as things don't always come as you expect them to.

Now look at your list. Are there any steps that you can take now towards getting some of these things? Formulate a plan for these steps and put the plans into action. There is always something you can do to work towards anything, and by putting out the right messages, you'll make the changes you need to make instead of the ones you don't need, and the things that you do want will present themselves to you. Opportunities to obtain more of your desires will then appear. Over time, you'll have more of what you do want, and your life will be greatly improved.

To help train your mind to think more positive there are many tools at your disposal. Using visualization meditations will help put a visual image in your mind and in turn, help it resonate the vibrations you wish to send out to attract back In addition to meditating and being aware of your thoughts, you can help your mind to attract what you want by writing affirmations and your goals and dreams on pieces of paper and placing them around your house. Place these reminders everywhere you can, and whenever you see them, read them and think about them with all your energy.

You can also make a vision board. On a poster, stick pictures of things you want, such as a car, a house, a holiday, or a bank statement showing millions of dollars in your account. Put the poster on the wall and take a minute to look at it every day, giving the pictures your energy. This will imprint what you want on your subconscious mind and make your intention more powerful.

Always pay attention to any ideas that come to you when you think about your goals. You may find a way to take a step closer to your goal.

To summarize, these are the steps for using the law of attraction:

1. Define what you don't want.
2. Define what you do want.
3. Focus on the things you want.
4. Take action to move towards what you want.
5. Pay attention to your thoughts.
6. Watch for opportunities to take more steps towards your desires.
7. Believe.
8. Trust.
9. Show gratitude.
10. Expect.
11. Enjoy the rewards!

You have just taken the first step towards improving your life. Life will be better from now on. Remember to believe and trust and stay positive. Read more books, listen to CDs, research, and learn.

Open your mind. I guarantee that if you apply these principles and your mind to improving your life, you will succeed.

Dreams

Everyone dreams, although we don't always remember our dreams. I've known some people who've claimed that they have never had a dream. This may be possible if they're not sleeping deeply enough to achieve the right brainwave activity during sleep for dreaming or if they have some condition that prevents them from dreaming, but this isn't the case for the vast majority of us. Our dreams can help us process events that happened in our waking life, and they can also give us insights into our future to help us prepare for things to come, but often, our dreams make no sense. Many people have trouble remembering their dreams, and if we do, we usually only remember a small portion of a dream.

Some people have very vivid dreams that become reality, like the dream has given them a glimpse into the future. Other times, dreams may review events from the recent past or it shows us something about someone we know. These types of dreams are rare for most of us, and in most dreams, things are not what they seem, as images are often symbols. For example, if you dream that you're in a house, that house can be a symbol of your life. If it's in good shape and the rooms are all well furnished and in good order, then your life is good at the moment. However, if a room is run-down or dirty, if the furniture is broken, or if the whole house is falling down, then this may signify problems in a particular area of your life or in your whole life if the whole house is run down.

Many books have been written about interpreting the symbols in dreams, and these sometimes ascribe different meanings to the same symbol. If I look up the meaning of something I saw in a dream, I refer to a few different books and take the meaning that connects best with me. These tools can help you find meaning in your dreams, but to interpret them most accurately, it's best to keep a dream diary, as doing so will allow you to see patterns and find your own meanings for symbols. Following a few rules will help you get the most out of journaling, and with a little practice, dream interpretation can be quite simple.

The first thing to do is to keep a pen and dream journal within reach of your bed so you can access it when you wake up. To more easily remember your dream, go to sleep with the intention of remembering your dream when you wake up. Then, when you do wake up, try not to move. Just lie still and review as much as you can remember about your dreams in your mind. Go through every detail you can. When you've done this, sit up and write your dream down in your journal while it's fresh in your mind. If you move before you go through this process, you'll likely forget a lot of the details, and you may have trouble remembering much at all. Once you've written out your dream, you can then look up the meanings of the items you remembered and fit the pieces together to find meaning for the dream as a whole. Make this a habit, and you'll be amazed at how much your dreams reveal.

When you look at your dreams more closely, you may find that you gain control over your dreams. Simply by being more aware of what's happening in your dreams. You may realize that you're dreaming in the moment, and when this happens, you'll be able to direct your dream. For example, if you don't like how a scene from your dream is played out, then you can do a retake and change what happens while you dream. This is called *lucid dreaming*, and it's very exciting to realize you're able to do this. If dream interpretation interests you, you can gain a lot from learning more about it, including more enjoyment from your dreams and fun finding their meanings.

Many times I've been able to relate things that have happened in real life back to a dream I had a few nights before. In some cases, exactly what I dreamed happened in real life, and in others, everything appeared in symbols, and I didn't understand their meaning until what the symbols represented happened.

For example, I remembered one unusual dream well when I woke up, and I told Stephen about it. I was in the woods and I saw a bear cub. I went over to the cub and was playing with it when a big bear, a parent of the cub, came out and joined us. The big bear was friendly, and I felt like I was part of the bear family. Then I walked with the two bears, and we came across farmers with pitchforks who were trying to kill us, but I put up a reflective shield around us and repelled the attacks. The bears and I then went into a building that felt special and then into a big room. Three witches were there, and they tried to attack us with spells and wands. But I put my hand out and blocked their attacks, and I felt a white light around the bears and me. We then walked past the witches, and then we were back outside in the woods. The bears looked at me and then walked off into the woods. Then, I was at home in the kitchen, and Fiona, Ian's ex, was there, and I folded her up like piece of paper and put her in the freezer near the bread.

This was all I remembered, but it was very vivid and I felt it had a special meaning, but I didn't know what. A few days later, I had to go to the Katoomba courthouse to appear as a witness for Ian in his custody case for his daughter with Fiona, Jemmiah. Fiona had been making all types of false claims about Ian, saying he was an unfit parent, but I knew Ian was a good man and a wonderful father to all of his children, as the three children he and I have all love him very much and have a great relationship with him. So, Ian had asked me to testify on his behalf and to relate my experiences with Fiona during the years that she and Ian were together.

When I was leaving to go to the courthouse, I put on a pair of dress boots, and in the first shoe, I found a fork! I took it out and then checked the other shoe, and I found a black tourmaline crystal. I have no idea how they got there, but I connected the fork to the pitchforks I saw in my dream and felt this was like a warning that I would be attacked. Black tourmaline is used for protection, so I popped the crystal into my bra over my heart and left.

At the courthouse, I walked into the waiting room outside the courtroom, and Fiona jumped out of her seat and started yelling at me, calling me a witch and saying I would burn in hell. She was quite dramatic. I sat down with Peta, Ian's girlfriend and a lovely lady, and we just ignored Fiona, and she sat back down.

Soon after, I was called in to testify and was placed on the stand. While I was on the stand, three lawyers questioned me for a total of about ninety minutes. They tried to twist my words and catch me off guard, describing many events from the past and questioning my honesty and integrity. I think I handled all of the questions really well, as I only had to be honest, but I really felt attacked. After leaving the courtroom, I became emotional, my emotions intensified when I told Stephen about the experience.

On the drive home from the Blue Mountains, I thought about the dream and related everything in it to the events of the day in court. Jemmiah was the little cub and Ian the big bear. Fiona was the farmers with the pitchforks, and the lawyers trying to attack me were the witches in the big room. But there was one thing from the dream that hadn't yet become a reality. When we arrived home, I wrote Fiona's name on a piece of paper, folded it up, put it in a small container of water, and placed it in the freezer near the bread. This is a practice that can block negative energy from a person, and I felt that my doing this to Fiona in the dream was a sign that I should do this to protect myself and my family.

This is just one of many dreams that I have been able to relate to events in my life. The more I notice my dreams, the more relevance they have to my life, and the more you pay attention to your dreams, the better you'll understand them and use this information for your benefit.

Our dreams help our minds process our lives and prepare us for coming events, and it is easy to remember your dreams if you have the intention to do so. So why not take advantage of this natural ability and use it to improve and help yourself and others?

Crystals and Gemstones

Crystals and semiprecious gemstones that are used for healing work come from one source: Nature. Created from earth, all these stones have gone through a geologic process on their way to their present form.

The energetic field of gemstones, including those that come from meteorites, is influenced by geometric structure, colour, and the vibration of its atoms, which are in constant motion and thus emit an energy signature, or frequency. The gemstone's colour and the interplay of this colour with light can play a dynamic role in the stone's healing energy, causing it to stimulate or purify or heal or have a calming influence or effect.

A strong magical connection has always existed between human beings and gems. Evidence that gemstones were used for healing and helping people has been found from as far back as the fourth millennium before Christ. Ancient Chinese, Egyptians, Sumerians, Greeks, and Romans, as well as shamans and medicine men and other traditional healers have used gemstones for healing in multiple ways. They've made them into powders or elixirs, worn them, and carried them or placed them on the body in ceremonies and rituals. This ancient knowledge has been passed down to our day and is re-emerging as holistic health and healing gains popularity.

One method in which crystals are used for healing is called crystal healing, in which crystals are placed on or around the body. In this method, the crystals clear those energies that don't serve us in the highest, thereby assisting the body to shift energy in the body so that it can heal.

The human body has a complex electromagnetic system, also known as a resonant vibrational energy field. Nature has created crystals to be perfect conductors of this electromagnetism, as they carry vibrations that activate certain centres within our electromagnetic field, positively affecting our entire body systems and, in turn, helping us to change our lives and the lives of those we encounter.

Crystals can also be used to block negative energy, attract abundance, enhance our connection to spirit, and activate, stimulate, restore, or calm our senses.

One of the most common ways to cleanse crystals is to place them in direct sunlight or the direct light of a full moon. Another method is to wash them in salt water, preferably fresh seawater, although a solution of sea salt in plain water will also work. Please note, however, that some gemstones and crystals may dissolve in water. A third method of cleansing is to hold a crystal or place it in front of you and, using your energetic belief and power, to say a prayer over them for your spirit guides and God to cleanse them and bless them.

I have a few crystal bibles at home, and I have learnt much about crystals from them and other sources over the years. I keep many crystals around my home, and I use others every day in different ways. There are many uses for crystals in your daily life, and they don't need to be large for you to benefit from their energies.

Chapter 7

A Practical Guide to Psychic Development

Everyone is psychic; this is a fact! We have all experienced moments when we have received information, had a feeling or a hunch, felt like we knew the answer before the question was asked, or used our intuition.

Like anything, the more you practice using your psychic abilities, the better you will be. Whether your interest in psychic development lie in deepening your spiritual understanding, becoming more psychic, or establishing or enhancing communication with your spirit guides, I hope that in sharing my beliefs and understanding of many spiritual topics, you will come away with some information that helps you to achieve your spiritual goals and use all your psychic abilities.

Deep within all people is the desire to discover, experience, and fully express their "God-Self," the highest spiritual part of themselves that is both the connection to and expression of God within. When we discover our unique spiritual path, we begin to bring our bodies, minds, and spirits into balance. As we walk our path, we live in a state of constant union with the highest source, from which we are empowered to live fully, with confidence, joy, and peace. From this place of wholeness, we are also able to effectively use our spiritual gifts and abilities to assist and empower others. Universal truths can be found on all paths and within all traditions. Wisdom is everywhere, and if only we are open, we can tap into it.

Working with others to empower them to discover and walk their unique path and to fully express their spiritual gifts is one of the greatest joys in my life. But work in this industry can be a tough road. The knowledge I and other psychics and mediums have cannot be proved or justified. Some hide what they do from the general public so they are not ridiculed, for we see the world with different eyes. However, we are just people that have a special understanding, and this gives us the responsibility to help, share with, and touch the hearts of many. We provide a connection to spirit through our messages and can bring back hope when all is lost.

We psychics can connect to some people better than others, and we don't always have the answers. We can misinterpret the information we receive or can get our wires crossed, but we don't need to be right or wrong, we don't need to win, we don't need to be the best. We just need to be who we are and to do the best we can. We can touch a heart, we can give hope, we can carry a message of inspiration and determination and persistence. We can remind others that love never dies.

It doesn't matter who we are or how we use our ability; all that matters is what is in our hearts and that we share it to restore the light for a client when all lights have gone and give help to that one person who seeks it.

As you develop your own psychic or mediumship abilities, the obstacles you may face are mostly in your mind. Not only do you need to trust and believe in your ability to pick up messages from your psychic senses, your guides, or spirits, but you also need to be able to distinguish between what your psychic senses are picking up and what your own thoughts and feelings are telling you, as the two are easy to confuse. Telling the difference takes time and practice and feedback from the people you're doing readings for so you can gauge how much of the information you're giving is correct.

Being a Psychic or Medium

A psychic is a person who receives information through their psychic senses about a person, a place, an object, or an event. Psychics can gain insights into the past, present, or future, and they can receive both general and specific details related to the person, place, object, or event. Psychics gather information through their psychic senses and from their guides. Some receive information through dreams, and some use psychic tools, such as cards or tea leaves, together with their own abilities.

A medium, on the other hand, is a person who is able to communicate with spirits, accessing information about those who died, about their lives, and about events in the lives of people the spirits are connected to. All mediums are psychic, but not all psychics are mediums, as mediums will often communicate with spirits directly in addition to using their other psychic abilities to best assist those they serve. The purpose of a medium is also to provide evidence of the continuation of life after the transition known as death and to pass on messages that validate the communication with a specific spirit by giving details about him or her and to then provide proof that the spirit still has an active and intelligent consciousness by describing what the spirit sees and knows from the lives of those he or she left behind. These messages give descriptions of past times together or of the living person's activities since the spirit passed. This is evidence of survival of spirit after death.

A medium's communication with spirit is not the same as talking to another person, although talking is possible. Usually, the communication happens psychically, and it is therefore much more complicated and even confusing. Everybody is capable of receiving information through their psychic senses, but many people's beliefs block this process. Therefore, the first step in becoming a medium yourself is to let go of any beliefs that would hinder you. Realize that anything is possible, and believe in spirit and believe in yourself.

The spirit is the life force/energy/soul of every living creature. It is within each of us, and it is unique to each of us. As it is within each of us we are all able to connect with it. When our bodies stop functioning and die, its energy is released but still exists, taking with it all of its experiences from life and many of its characteristics. A medium can really feel a spirit's personality; however, his or her emotions are usually much more neutral than a living person's. I've known spirits to express grief and show empathy, and they can be angry, cheeky, funny, and mischievous, but the strongest emotions I feel when I connect with most spirits are peace and love. It is beautiful to feel these emotions, and I feel so happy when spirits connect with me like this.

Everything in the universe—humans, animals, plants, rocks, spirits—is made up of energy. This energy cannot be created or destroyed; it simply changes form. Energies vibrate at different rates, so if one energy force is to communicate with another, they must vibrate at similar rates. As we humans live in bodies, our vibrational energy is at a much lower frequency than that of spirit, so for communication to take place between the psychical and spiritual, the physical energy must raise its vibration and the spiritual energy must slow its vibration. To raise your energy to the level required for communication with spirit, you need to focus the conscious mind to allow your subconscious mind to receive information. You need to be aware of everything that is happening in your body through all of your senses. Meditation can help train your mind for this process.

Because spirits don't have psychical bodies, they can't speak or make gestures, so they instead communicate using telepathy, impressing thoughts, sounds, visions, and feelings into the mind and body of the medium. The medium may pick up messages from just one or from all of your psychic senses, but to do so, the medium must clear his or her mind of all excess chatter and remain open to receiving any and all energy impressions. Learn to let go of what you think about anything you receive. Do not judge; just accept. Turn off your tendency to figure things out with logic. The mind should simply recognize information as it comes in and record it.

The next step is to accurately interpret the information coming through. Sometimes the information will be very clear, so you'll know exactly what it is. At other times, it can come in bits and pieces, and interpreting it can be like solving a puzzle. Even when the medium puts the information in order, it may still make no sense to him or her but will make perfect sense to the client having the reading, so a medium needs feedback from the client in order to know if he or she is interpreting the information the right way. Sometimes a simple yes or no may be enough, but more details are often of more help to a medium in figuring out what the message means and giving clearer information. However, clients shouldn't feel that the medium is pushing them for too much information, as that may make them feel that a medium is only telling them what they've said and not what spirit says, giving the reading little impact.

The greatest challenge for psychics or mediums is to recognize how they pick up the information and then how to interpret the information and convey a meaningful message, as they must be familiar with how their psychic senses work. However, the more mediums and psychics work with their senses, the better they become at understanding them.

The imagination is also very important to a medium, as spirits are capable of connecting with us and imprinting thoughts into that part of the mind. Many people believe that a connection to spirit is all in the imagination, but the truth is that only some of it is imagination; most is actual communication. Experience allows the medium to tell the difference between the two most of the time. So, allow your imagination to work with spirit and trust in what you receive.

There are many pitfalls to intuitive communication, and your own attitude may be the biggest one. You can be your own worst critic, and this attitude won't help your development. Instead, have a positive attitude, believe you can do it, and trust in your abilities. Let go of any doubt. You may find it helpful to write down any of your negative beliefs that are holding you back. Once you've done this, write out positive statements that counteract those beliefs. This process of consciously reversing your negative beliefs can help you achieve success in any area of your life, as articulating positivity in this way gives it the power to overcome any negativity.

Mediums and psychics can pick up information from spirits, spirit guides, angels, or the universal pool of knowledge, where all knowledge is stored in a collective mind like a library. Since everything is connected, all you need to do is ask for the information you seek, and it will be made available for you to pick up through your psychic senses. When using these senses, let go of what you think and record what comes in without censorship. Be positive and practice.

Meditation

Meditation has many benefits if it's practised regularly, including relaxation, the ease of tension, improvements in health, better sleep, the ability to work through personal problems from the past and present, the development of psychic abilities, a connection to guidance from other realms, and contact with your inner self. Meditation is the key to unlocking amazing possibilities. One of the main functions of meditation is to still the conscious mind to allow the subconscious more room and time to do its thing. This can be done by focusing the conscious mind on one thing and not allowing it to flit about among thoughts, using intense thinking to sort through stuff subconsciously.

There are many different ways to meditate, and you should experiment with a few different methods until you find what suits you the best, and I recommend practising a few different types of meditation regularly. Visualization is an important part of many types of meditation. Some people find that they have trouble visualizing anything very well at first, and if you find that's the case for you, try practicing visualization exercises, such as the one below. Reciting mantras, focusing the mind on a single sound, or concentrating on the breathing can also be quite effective, and structured meditations and unstructured meditations employ these techniques.

Visualization Exercise. Place an object such as a candle or an apple or a coloured piece of paper on a table and sit in front of it. Stare at the object and observe it in detail. When you feel that you know every detail about the object, close your eyes and picture the object. If you can't see the whole thing with your mind's eye, then think about a detail of it. If that doesn't work, then open your eyes and stare at the object again, repeating the exercise until you can form an image of the whole object in your mind. When you have done this, try replacing the object with something else and start over. Your mind will soon be able to visualize at will.

The breath is very important when you meditate, and breathing properly will help you gain the most from your meditation. It is best to breathe in through your nose, expanding your diaphragm fully, and then out through your mouth. To make sure you're doing this correctly, stand up and place your hands on your ribs at the base of your sternum with your fingertips just touching each other. Then, take in a deep breath, allowing your chest to expand. Your fingertips should separate an inch or more when your lungs are full. Practice doing this until you get used to this style of breathing.

Whenever you feel unbalanced, you can ground and balance yourself with this breathing exercise: Block one nostril and breathe in through the other nostril. Then, open the first nostril and block the other and breathe out. Now breathe in using the same nostril, switch which nostril is blocked, and breathe out of the other nostril. Continue this cycle of breathing in and out about ten times.

Your mind will wander while you meditate, at times this is a good thing, especially during visualization. It's important to notice every thought that comes to mind as you meditate, as you may receive important revelations. However, other meditations require you to focus your mind on one thing and let go of any other thoughts. To do this, you must be aware when you have stopped focusing and your thoughts have drifted. Simply acknowledge the thoughts that come, and then let them go, and refocus your mind. If you do this every time you've stopped focusing, you'll soon be able to focus for longer periods, and by meditating regularly, you'll become more aware of your thoughts and your surroundings, noticing more detail with all of your senses.

Visualization meditations can help you to connect with your guides and with spirits who can help you sort through issues and give you insights into the future and past, including past lives. Visualization meditations also allow you to have amazing experiences such as astral travel. You can visualize yourself transforming into animals or even into water so you can experience what it's like to be a pond, a river, a lake, the ocean, or even rain. You can also use visualization meditations for healing and to enhance the law of attraction by seeing yourself with the things you want in order to attract these things to you.

Focusing meditations are a great way to enhance your ability to concentrate and to more easily let go, which can be especially beneficial when going to sleep, as you can more easily let go of thoughts which would normally keep you awake.

You don't have to sit by yourself in a dark room to meditate Any task that allows your conscious mind to focus on one thing or one train of thought can be a meditation, including working, walking, or even driving your car, but sitting or lying quietly and not moving is most beneficial. All you really need to do is to stop your mind from wandering. When your conscious mind can stay focused on what you're doing, your subconscious mind can take more control.

In this way, the subconscious can tap into all that is within and without, all the energy and knowledge of the universe and all that is spiritual and physical. To gain the most benefit from meditation, begin by asking yourself what you would like to achieve, and choose a meditation to suit that intention.

Practice makes perfect, so don't expect too much too soon. If you go at your own pace, before you know it, you'll notice differences in your life. With a little discipline, you'll quickly improve your meditation and will be able to meditate for longer periods. Ideally, you should meditate every day.

I recommend that at first you meditate for only about ten minutes, as forcing yourself into an hour-long meditation when you've just begun will only leave you frustrated. When your mind becomes accustomed to relaxing and focusing, you can then increase the time. When you become skilled at basic meditation, you can build your practice to open your chakras, balance your energy, meet your spirit guide, visit past live's, travel in the astral realm, and do much more.

You can meditate anywhere, even in a crowed and noisy area, once you're skilled at it, but to begin with, find a place where you'll be comfortable and undisturbed. If you live with other people, ask them not to bother you during your meditation unless there's an emergency, and keep your pets out of the room, too. Turn off your telephone as well. Set up your meditation area so you can sit comfortably, and decorate it with positive things you like. Dim the lights, light some candles, and play soothing, soft music, which will help you focus and drown out noisy neighbours, barking dogs, traffic, or other background noises. Sit upright whether in a chair or cross-legged on the floor or lie on the floor, although some find reclining not very effective, as it's too easy to fall asleep. Remember to Breathe deeply from your diaphragm with your full lung capacity throughout the meditation.

As you begin meditating, you may like to create an image in your mind of a place where you feel safe and comfortable. This could be a spot in nature with lush vegetation, waterfalls, statues, and soft grass; a building full of rooms for specific issues; or a tropical island. It's up to you!

You can begin your practice by finding a routine that helps you to relax your body and mind. I like to start at my head and relax all of my muscles one by one down to my toes. I then visualize sending roots out from my feet or the base of my spine to ground me and connect me to the energy of the earth. I then draw red energy from it up into my body and let it radiate throughout my body. I then bring in white light from above into the top of my head and draw that energy throughout my body, allowing it to mix with the energy from the earth until it overflows from my body and into my aura. I then form a pink energy bubble around myself to protect me during the rest of the meditation.

Visualize this in as much detail as possible. Notice whether it's daytime or night-time. See the leaves on the trees or the sand on the beach. Notice how the water moves or whether it is still.

Notice whether the walls of the cave are rock or clay or another substance. Look all around you, and see everything that you can in your safe place. Take in all its beauty.

Once you have the picture in your mind, incorporate your other senses. Feel the air on your skin. Is it warm or cool? Is there a breeze? Feel the sun on your face and the sand or earth or leaves or water below you. Smell the air. Does it smell salty or fresh? What other fragrances do you smell? Hear everything the rushing water, the wind in the treetops, the rustle of animals and birds.

Stay in this safe place for as long as you wish. You may see animals or people, your guides or angels. Notice how they react to you. Talk to them if you can or if you feel like it. Don't worry if they don't respond at first. Sometimes spirit guides like to check you out for a while before they talk to you. If you don't see anyone, that's fine, too. Maybe you just need to be alone in this place.

When you are ready to return, begin noticing the things in your meditation area: feel the chair or ground beneath you; listen to the sounds around you; become aware of your heartbeat and your breathing and the rest of your body again (it may have gone numb), and release any attachments you made while meditating. When you're fully aware of things around you, slowly open your eyes and sit quietly for a minute or two.

Then, drink some water or tea and eat a bite of cheese or bread. This will help anchor you in this plane and ground you so that you don't feel drained or jittery.

You can also meditate with a recorded guided meditation, a book, or in a group class. I suggest you try them all.

The following are a basic focusing meditation and a visualization meditation to get you started.

Breathing Meditation

Sit comfortably in a chair with your spine straight, your feet flat on the floor, and your hands relaxed on your lap. Now close your eyes and relax every part of your body. Breathe deeply. Inhale through your nose, and exhale through your mouth. With each breath, feel yourself relax more deeply. Focus on each part of your body one by one, starting with the top of your head. Feel the tension drain away from the muscles in your face, relax, your lips, your cheeks, and your jaw. Relax your neck and shoulders. Feel the tension drain away from your arms and your hands, relax. Release all of your anxiety in your chest, in your back, in your stomach, relax. Let go of all of your worries. Relax your hips, thighs, calves, and feet, feeling the tension fall away. Your entire body is now relaxed and heavy. With each breath, feel yourself relax more, inhale through your nose and exhale through your mouth.

Visualize yourself sitting in a room, completely relaxed. Imagine roots growing from your feet, connecting you to the earth, grounding you. Imagine the roots reaching deep into the earth. Send them down as far as you can. When you're ready, draw the energy of the earth up through the roots. This energy is red. Feel the red energy rise from the earth and through your feet, up your legs, and into your body until it reaches your core.

Now imagine the roof above you disappearing or lifting off. See a brilliant white light come down from above and enter your head.

Feel this light as it travels down your body and into your core. Feel the light fill you up, penetrating every cell in your body.

Allow the red energy from the earth to mix with the white energy from above to create a soft pink energy. Allow this energy to fill your body, entering every cell and radiating outwards until it overflows from your body and fills the air surrounding you. See how it forms a pink energy bubble around your body, fills your aura, and pushes away all negativity from within and around you. This energy bubble will protect you from negativity and harm.

Now return your focus to your breath. Inhale through the nose, hold. Exhale out the mouth, hold. Breathe in one, two, three. Hold one, two, three. Breathe out one, two, three. Hold one, two, three.

Continue breathing in this way for five minutes, or more as you build up over time. If you notice that your mind has wandered to a thought, acknowledge the thought, let it go, and bring your focus back to your breathing.

Now take your focus away from breath, place the roof back over your head. Feel the roots release from your feet. Wiggle your toes, and focus on your body. You should feel very relaxed and calm. Give thanks and feel grateful for everything. Feel the tingles and twitches as your body takes control. Feel grounded. Feel how relaxed and calm you are. Stretch your muscles. Finally, gradually open your eyes and bring your focus back to your surroundings.

Visualization Meditation: The Farm

Sit comfortably in a chair with your spine straight, your feet flat on the floor, and your hands relaxed on your lap. Now close your eyes and relax every part of your body. Breathe deeply. Inhale through your nose, and exhale through your mouth. With each breath, feel yourself relax more deeply. Focus on each part of your body one by one, starting with the top of your head. Feel the tension drain away from the muscles in your face, relax, your lips, your cheeks, and your jaw. Relax your neck and shoulders. Feel the tension drain away from your arms and your hands, relax. Release all of your anxiety in your chest, in your back, in your stomach, relax. Let go of all of your worries. Relax your hips, thighs, calves, and feet, feeling the tension fall away. Your entire body is now relaxed and heavy. With each breath, feel yourself relax more, inhale through your nose and exhale through your mouth.

Visualize yourself sitting in a room, completely relaxed. Imagine roots growing from your feet, connecting you to the earth, grounding you. Imagine the roots reaching deep into the earth. Send them down as far as you can. When you're ready, draw the energy of the earth up through the roots. This energy is red. Feel the red energy rise from the earth and through your feet, up your legs, and into your body until it reaches your core.

Now imagine the roof above you disappearing or lifting off. See a brilliant white light come down from above and enter your head. Feel this light as it travels down your body and into your core. Feel the light fill you up, penetrating every cell in your body.

Allow the red energy from the earth to mix with the white energy from above to create a soft pink energy. Allow this energy to fill your body, entering every cell and radiating outwards until it overflows from your body and fills the air surrounding you. See how it forms a pink energy bubble around your body, fills your aura, and pushes away all negativity from within and around you. This energy bubble will protect you from negativity and harm.

When you are ready, take in a deep breath, and as you exhale, relax your entire body. Take long, slow breaths, slowing your heart rate, allowing your entire body to relax more and even more relaxed, until you're so relaxed you can't feel your body. Take calm, peaceful, long, slow breaths.

Now visualize yourself in the countryside on a farm. Trees laden with all kinds of ripe fruit surround fields filled with all different types of lush, green vegetables. See pastures on which sheep and cows graze and a pond where ducks and swans swim. Look to the top of a nearby hill and see a beautiful white building with arches and stained-glass windows. Listen. Hear music in the distance, like a choir of angels gently humming.

Look around and see a path leading to the building. Make your way to it, and when you reach it, notice that it's paved with marble, smooth and polished. About every one hundred metres are seats, and statues beside the pathway here and there. Step onto the marble pathway and walk towards the building on the hill. Look out over the farm and notice huge sheds and massive silos. Everything is in abundance here. Everything is thriving.

Suddenly along the path, there is a statue that looks out of place. It is a figure of someone suffering. Take a moment to sit in the seat across from the statue and concentrate on the statue. Think of times in your life when you've suffered, when you've felt pain. Remember the events, and feel the emotions again.

Now hear the angels humming again. See before you a bright light. It is an angel who has come to take your suffering and pain. Give them to her, and allow her to replace them with love. Now see that the statue across from you has changed. It is smiling and is no longer in pain.

Give thanks for this blessing, stand, and continue up the pathway. See that there are now crystals, of all types the size of boulders sitting along the path every twenty metres or so. Look out over the farm again and see people working, collecting the bounty of Mother Nature, tending to irrigating, weeding, feeding, collecting, packing, and all of the farm work. Look more closely at one of the workers and see their wings. All the workers form an army of angels, ready to provide you with whatever you need.

Turn back to the path and see another statue that looks out of place. Take a seat and notice that the statue is broken. It looks sad and lost. Allow it to remind you of a time when you've felt broken or lost, hurt or sad. Feel these emotions again.

Hear the angels singing, and see a bright light before you and a beautiful angel looks at you with rich blue eyes. As she reaches out, give her these emotions, and feel the love coming from her like waves of warm tingles. Look up at the statue again and see the statue that it is fixed and smiling.

Get up again and continue walking up the hill. As you get closer to the building, notice that the pathway is more beautiful. Sweet-smelling flowers are everywhere. A sign along the path reads, "Everything is abundant in the universe. Simply think abundantly about the things you want, and you will attract them to you in abundance." Think about this message for a minute.

Now continue along the path again and look out at the flowers and crystals and statues and seats. Not far to go now to the building at the top of the hill. The flowers are so bright, and you feel relaxed and blissful.

You see another statue that looks out of place. It is a small child who looks afraid. Take a seat and think about what you are afraid of, what fear is stopping you from achieving or obtaining or choosing. Here the humming of the angels again, and see a bright white light and then an angel. This time, the angel leaves your fears with you but gives you courage to get past them. See that the statue of the frightened child has been replaced by the statue of a brave warrior.

Stand up and again continue along the path. Finally, reach the top of the hill and look out over the farm. See it stretch for miles in all directions. On another hillside, see a three-story mansion with lush gardens surrounding it.

Turn now to the building in front, and see that it is carved out of white marble. It's spectacular, with high arches over the door and windows. The sun reflects off the white marble and makes the building glow. You see a crystal seat in a crystal arch near the entrance on which a sign rests that says, "Sit here." Make your way to the seat and sit down. Feel a tingling through your body as the crystal's vibrations change the energy in your body, cleansing and purifying your body, pulling out negative patterns and energy and transforming your body, bringing it into harmony, curing any illness. A brilliant white light flashes before you and glows pink, green, and then gold. The angel from the path smiles down at you. Feel the love coming from her, feel her energy healing your body, restoring you to full health. Feel an abundance of energy, happiness, and contentment.

Get up now and go to the entrance. On the door is a sign that reads, "Whatever you desire, focus in your mind, believe in your heart, trust in yourself, and pursue it with love."

Walk inside and see the sunlight shining through the stained-glass windows, and coloured lights dance on the marble walls. Look down at piles of gold and jewels on the floor. Turn to see a stack of money ten feet high and a big round sofa with fluffy cushions in the middle of the room and a small table laden with grapes, nuts, and wine. Pour yourself a small drink and relax on the sofa.

Now think about something you want. This can be a change you would like to make in your life, something you want to have, something you want to do, or something you'd like to create in the near future. Focus only on that one thing, whether it be; more money, more time, more love, or something that will make you happier. You are sitting in the temple of abundance, so whatever you focus on in here will manifest in your real life in the near future. Think carefully about what you want, how will it affect you, and who else it will affect. Think about what steps you could take to obtain what you want. Consider how you would feel if you had it now. What would it mean to you? How grateful would you feel to have it? How good does it make you feel?

You cannot be greedy, as there is more than enough for everyone to have as much as they like. You deserve to have it. It is given to you with love. You can create this in your life now!

With another flash of white light, the angel appears once more. Feel her arms wrap around you and squeeze you tight. Feel how safe and protected, warm and loved, comforted and blessed you are.

Then say goodbye to the angel, and give her your gratitude and love. Get up off the sofa and leave the building. Once you're back outside, notice a sign that says, "All that is here and all that is there is here for everyone, for all to share." Walk back down the path and think about what an exciting time you've had. Notice the statues, the crystals, the angels. Feel excited about creating and attracting something new into your life.

When you are ready, concentrate once more on your breathing. Take long, slow breaths in and out. Focus on your body. Feeling how relaxed and happy you are. Visualize yourself back in your seat in your meditation room. Feel the roots release from your feet. Give thanks to the earth for its energy, and send your love, appreciation, and respect to the planet. Give thanks to God for the abundance, love, and blessings you receive. Replace the roof over the room, and sever all attachments to any negativity in your life. Think about your thoughts, and keep a positive attitude. Know that you are in control and can create a better life for yourself by being more positive.

Choose to focus your energy on love and happiness.

When you are ready, wiggle your toes and stretch your muscles. Feeling very relaxed, you can now open your eyes.

Chakras and Your Energy System

Chakras are the energy portals in your body, that draw in the energy of different types, including colour, to various parts of the body. *Chakra* is a Sanskrit word which means "wheel," which indicates a chakra's spinning vortex. Some traditions believe that the human body contains hundreds of chakras that are the key to the operation of our being. These spinning wheels draw in coded information—anything from a colour's vibration to an ultraviolet ray to a microwave to another person's energy (that's why other people's moods have an effect on us!)—and, in essence receive the health of the surrounding environment. Our chakras also radiate our internal energy.

Of these hundreds of chakras, we have seven main chakras, each connected to the physical, emotional, mental, and spiritual parts of our being. On the physical level, each of these seven chakras governs an organ or gland, which, in turn, is connected to other body parts that resonate at the same frequency.

Each chakra and the organ, gland, and body system it's connected to is associated with the vibrational frequency of a particular colour. For example, the heart chakra governs the thymus gland, the heart, lungs, bronchial system, lymph glands, secondary circulatory system, immune system, and the arm and hands and resonates with the colour green.

The seven main chakra centres are aligned along the spinal column. If the body experiences a disturbance on any level, this will manifest in the chakra's vitality. To balance a chakra emotionally, intellectually, physically, or spiritually, we need to bring in the chakra's colour vibration. When one part of a chakra centre is out of sync—overactive, underactive, or blocked—it eventually affects its other parts and its neighbouring chakra. The imbalance will be felt mentally, emotionally, or physically.

What Is Energy, and How Does It Affect Our Chakras?

The sun is our main source of light, heat, and energy. Not only does sunlight sustain all life on Earth but also the Earth itself. It provides plants with the energy for photosynthesis, which in turn sustains the lives of all animals, including humans. Sunlight consists of energy in the form of the electromagnetic waves and part of this electromagnetic energy includes cosmic rays, gamma rays, X-rays, visible light, infrared rays, microwaves, and short and long radio waves. We use many of these energies in our daily lives; however, we seem not to put much emphasis on visible light. By holding a prism towards the sun, we can break down the visible spectrum of light rays into seven different beams of colour, or colour energies: red, orange, yellow, green, blue, indigo, and violet. We can see these seven colours in a rainbow, a drop of rain or dew, and even in a snowflake.

Colour and light are inseparable. Each colour in the spectrum of visible light is a wave with a different wavelength and frequency and affects us differently. Red has the longest wavelength and the slowest frequency, and we innately recognize it as warm and stimulating. Violet has the shortest wavelength and the fastest frequency, and we recognize it as cool and calming. We perceive colours when light enters our eyes and stimulates the rod and cone retinal cells. These cells send electrical impulses through the optic nerve to the visual cortex of the brain, and we see colour. Before the impulses reach the brain, they pass through the pituitary gland, which in turn triggers other glands in various parts of the body to secrete hormones. Many body functions and their associated chakras are, therefore, stimulated or retarded by different colours.

Since light physically affects glands and hormones, it has a marked influence on our moods and feelings. Certain colours can calm the mind while others can stimulate it. We need light energy to nourish our emotions and our physical bodies, including our brains and our chakras. Light can also enter the body through our skin and our breath, and we can receive additional colour energy through foods, herbs, vitamins, sounds, minerals, crystals, clothing, and decor.

Importance of Our Chakra System

In reality, little is understood about the human psyche and its intricate systems. However, medical science has proven that toxins and other impurities, including negative thoughts, chemicals in our food, and poor environmental factors, influence our bodies. Constant exposure to such pollution can cause imbalances in our chakras, which can affect us on a physical level. Since western and traditional health care systems at this time may be unable to totally cure our imbalances, it is up to us as individuals to improve our own health and to consider that we may be our own best doctors, and understanding the chakra system may help you improve your own physical, emotional, spiritual, and mental health. No one is totally responsible for you except you!

When all parts of you (all seven chakra centres) are communicating equally and working in harmony with each other as a unified whole, you will have no energy disorders. In other words, if the mental, physical, emotional, and spiritual parts of you are equally strong and working in alliance, you will function at your optimum level.

We live in such a fast-paced world that we often forget about functioning as a whole being, and put too much emphasis on the independence of parts of our health and very little on their interdependence. Our chakras are interdependent and must remain in harmony and balance for optimum health.

Your mind alone cannot nurture your whole being, and eating a proper diet cannot solve all your problems. You must take care of the whole you to keep your house in order.

To understand your chakra system, then you must learn what each chakra's function is and how it represents a part of your whole being.

The Root or Base Chakra

- o Red
- o Located at the base of the spine, this chakra is associated with survival, vitality, grounding, stability, reality, support, courage, individuality, sexuality, and impulsiveness.
- o Imbalances manifest as fatigue, lower back pain, sciatic nerve pain, anaemia, depression, and cold and flu.
- o Stimulants include physical exercise, sexual activity, restful sleep, gardening, creative activities, working with your hands, red foods and drinks, red gemstones, red clothing, and red oils such as sandalwood or ylang-ylang.

Sacral Chakra

- o Orange
- o Located just below the navel, this chakra is associated with emotions, intimacy, sensuality, procreation, polarity, confidence, sociability, freedom, and movement.
- o Imbalances manifest as eating disorders, drug and alcohol abuse, depression, asthma, allergies, yeast infections, urinary problems, and sensuality issues.

o   Stimulants include aromatherapy, massage and sensual
    touch, orange foods and drinks, orange gemstones, orange
    clothing, and orange oils such as melissa or orange (the
    citrus fruit).

Solar Plexus

o   Yellow
o   Located above the navel, this chakra is associated with
    knowledge, will, personal power, wit, humour, laughter,
    mental clarity, optimism, self-control, curiosity, and
    awareness.
o   Imbalances manifest as digestive problems, ulcers,
    diabetes, constipation, nervousness, toxicity, parasites,
    and poor memory.
o   Stimulants include yellow foods and drinks, yellow
    gemstones, yellow clothing, and yellow oils such as lemon
    or lemongrass.

Heart Chakra

o   Green
o   Located in the centre of your chest, this chakra is associated
    with relationships, love, acceptance, compassion, guilt,
    forgiveness, harmony, peace, and growth.
o   Imbalances manifest as heart and breathing disorders,
    chest pain, high blood pressure, immune system problems,
    and muscle tension.
o   Stimulants include nature walks, spending time with
    family and friends, green foods and drinks, green
    gemstones, green clothing, and green oils such as
    eucalyptus or pine.

Throat Chakra

o Blue
o Located in the throat, this chakra is associated with communication, speech, trust, wisdom, creative expression, planning, organization, and caution.
o Imbalances manifest as swollen glands; thyroid imbalances; fevers; infections; bloating; mouth, jaw, tongue, neck, and shoulder problems; hyperactivity; hormonal disorders; and mood swings.
o Stimulants include singing, poetry, meaningful conversations, art, blue foods and drinks, blue clothing, blue gemstones, and blue oils such as chamomile or geranium.

Brow or Third Eye Chakra

o Indigo
o Located between the eyes on the forehead, this chakra is associated with intuition, invention, psychic abilities, perception, understanding, self-realization, release, memory, and fearlessness.
o Imbalances manifest as spaceyness, forgetfulness, headaches, poor eyesight, tension, poor concentration, and sleep disorders.
o Stimulants include stargazing, meditation, indigo foods and drinks, indigo gemstones, indigo clothing, and indigo oils such as patchouli or frankincense.

Crown Chakra

o Violet
o Located on the top of the head, this chakra relates to knowledge, wisdom, inspiration, charisma, awareness, self-sacrifice, the higher self, and vision.

o   Imbalances manifest as headaches, photosensitivity, mental illness, epilepsy, skin rashes, varicose veins, senility, brain disorders, and confusion.

o   Stimulants include focusing on dreams and goals; planning for the future; violet foods, drinks, and gemstones; violet clothing; and violet oils such as jasmine or lavender.

Chakra-Balancing Meditation

Sit comfortably in a chair with your spine straight, your feet flat on the floor, and your hands relaxed on your lap. Now close your eyes and relax every part of your body. Breathe deeply. Inhale through your nose, and exhale through your mouth. With each breath, feel yourself relax more deeply. Focus on each part of your body one by one, starting with the top of your head. Feel the tension drain away from the muscles in your face, relax, your lips, your cheeks, and your jaw. Relax your neck and shoulders. Feel the tension drain away from your arms and your hands, relax. Release all of your anxiety in your chest, in your back, in your stomach, relax. Let go of all of your worries. Relax your hips, thighs, calves, and feet, feeling the tension fall away. Your entire body is now relaxed and heavy. With each breath, feel yourself relax more, inhale through your nose and exhale through your mouth.

Visualize yourself sitting in a room, completely relaxed. Imagine roots growing from your feet, connecting you to the earth, grounding you. Imagine the roots reaching deep into the earth. Send them down as far as you can. When you're ready, draw the energy of the earth up through the roots. This energy is red. Feel the red energy rise from the earth and through your feet, up your legs, and into your body until it reaches your core.

Now imagine the roof above you disappearing or lifting off. See a brilliant white light come down from above and enter your head. Feel this light as it travels down your body and into your core. Feel the light fill you up, penetrating every cell in your body.

Allow the red energy from the earth to mix with the white energy from above to create a soft pink energy. Allow this energy to fill your body, entering every cell and radiating outwards until it overflows from your body and fills the air surrounding you. See how it forms a pink energy bubble around your body, fills your aura, and pushes away all negativity from within and around you. This energy bubble will protect you from negativity and harm.

Focus on your base chakra, located near the base of your spine. Visualize the colour red, and hold it in your mind. See the colour start spinning like a bright red lotus flower, creating a swirling red vortex that opens wider and wider, spinning faster and faster until your base chakra is open all the way.

Now focus on your sacral chakra, located below the navel. Visualize the colour orange, and hold it in your mind. See the colour start spinning like a bright orange lotus flower, creating a swirling orange vortex that opens wider and wider, spinning faster and faster until your sacral chakra is open all the way.

Now focus on your solar plexus, located above the navel below the ribs. Visualize the colour yellow, and hold it in your mind. See the colour start spinning like a bright yellow lotus flower, creating a swirling yellow vortex that opens wider and wider, spinning faster and faster until your solar plexus chakra is open all the way.

Now focus on your heart chakra, located in the centre of the chest. Visualize the colour green, and hold it in your mind. See the colour start spinning like a bright green lotus flower, creating a swirling green vortex that opens wider and wider, spinning faster and faster until your heart chakra is open all the way.

Now focus on your throat chakra, located in your throat. Visualize the colour blue, and hold it in your mind. See the colour start spinning like a bright blue lotus flower, creating a swirling blue vortex that opens wider and wider, spinning faster and faster until your throat chakra is open all the way.

Now focus on your third eye chakra, located on your forehead. Visualize the colour indigo, and hold it in your mind. See the colour start spinning like a bright indigo lotus flower, creating a swirling indigo vortex that opens wider and wider, spinning faster and faster until your third eye chakra is open all the way.

Now focus on your crown chakra, located at the top of your head. Visualize the colour violet, and hold it in your mind. See the colour start spinning like a bright violet lotus flower, creating a swirling violet vortex that opens wider and wider, spinning faster and faster until your crown chakra is open all the way.

All of your chakras are open, and energy flows into your body on all levels, reaches your core, and radiates to every organ and cell in your body. Focus on this energy. Feel it resonating within you. Bring a ball of this energy through your solar plexus and into your energy field in front of you. Look at it. Can you see the colours within this energy? Slowly send this ball of energy around your body through your energy field. Send it up past all of your chakras, over your head, and bring it back down behind you around your body, and back up in front of you, past all your chakras. Keep this energy moving around your body, flowing smoothly past all your chakras.

Take notice of any differences you feel as it goes past each chakra. Does it slow down and feel heavier, or does it speed up and feel lighter? Does it jump or skip? At which chakras do you feel the flow is impeded?

As this energy flows past each chakra, allow it to cleanse and balance it, as though it were an energy brush. Take notice of which chakras may need extra stimulation after the meditation. Make a mental note as the energy flows around your body. Stay focused on the energy, and spend a moment cleansing and balancing your chakras.

When you're ready, bring this ball of energy to a stop in front of you. Take another look at it. Does it look different than it did before? Is it cloudy? Send this energy upwards and release it to the universe.

Spend a moment now to close down your chakras. Start with the crown chakra. Picture the spinning violet vortex slowing, closing, and the lotus flower coming into focus. Visualize the flower petals closing tightly.

Now move down to the third eye chakra. Picture the spinning indigo vortex slowing, closing, and the lotus flower coming into focus. Visualize the flower petals closing tightly.

Now down to the throat chakra. Picture the spinning blue vortex slowing, closing, and the lotus flower coming into focus. Visualize the flower petals closing tightly.

Now down to the heart chakra. Picture the spinning green vortex slowing, closing, and the lotus flower coming into focus. Visualize the flower petals closing tightly.

Now down to the solar plexus chakra. Picture the spinning yellow vortex slowing, closing, and the lotus flower coming into focus you see the lotus flower slowing down. Visualize the flower petals closing tightly.

Now down to the sacral chakra. Picture the spinning orange vortex slowing, closing, and the lotus flower coming into focus. Visualize the flower petals closing tightly.

Now down to the base chakra. Picture the spinning red vortex slowing, closing, and the lotus flower coming into focus. Visualize the flower petals closing tightly.

All of your chakras are now closed. Give thanks and gratitude.

Now bring your focus to your body. You should feel very relaxed and calm. Feel the tingles and twitches as your body takes control. Feel the roots let go from your feet and go back into the earth. Wiggle your toes. Feel grounded. Place the roof back over your head, stretch your muscles, and gradually open your eyes and bring your focus back to your surroundings.

Use this meditation or a similar chakra meditation regularly to balance and cleanse your chakras. Pay attention during the meditation to any chakras that may need additional stimulation to work at their optimum level. Other methods of cleansing and balancing your chakras include using the acoustic vibrations of tuning forks, bells, or chants or using crystals, pendulums, coloured lights.

Psychic Senses

Most psychic senses are an extension of your five physical senses: sight, sound, touch, taste, and smell. The following describes these psychic senses:

- *Clairvoyance*, or "clear seeing," is the ability to see objects, animals, people, or anything else that is not physically present. This sight occurs in the mind's eye. Some mediums say that this is a natural visual state, while others say that they must train their minds to use this sense with practices as meditation or with assistance from spiritual helpers. Some clairvoyant mediums can see a spirit as though the spirit has a physical body and were physically present. Other mediums see the spirit in as though it were in a movie, a television programme, or still picture in their minds.
- *Clairaudience*, or "clear hearing," is the ability to hear the voices or thoughts of spirits. Some mediums hear these as though they're listening to a person near them talking to them, but others mediums hear the voices in their minds as verbal thoughts.
- *Clairsentience*, or "clear sensing" or "clear feeling," is the ability to feel an impression of what a spirit wants to communicate or to feel sensations in the body instilled by a spirit. A clairsentient medium may take on the ailments of a spirit, feeling the physical problem the spirit suffered before death.
- *Clairalience*, or "clear smelling," is the ability to smell a spirit. For example, a medium may smell the pipe tobacco of a person who smoked during life.

- *Clairgustance,* or "clear tasting," is the ability to receive taste impressions from a spirit.
- *Claircognizance,* or "clear knowing," is the ability to know something without receiving it through the other physical or psychic senses. It is a feeling that one just knows. Often, a psychic will claim to have the feeling that a message or situation is right or wrong.

When you use your psychic abilities, surrender any expectations you hold about what you or your client want and just accept the information that comes in through your senses. A medium should be open to whatever spirits show up to pass on messages; we cannot pick and choose who we wish to hear from, although we may put out the intention that we want to hear from a particular spirit. Also, there are no guarantees you will hear what you want to hear or get the answers you are hoping for.

Simply honour the messages that come through and pass them on. Keep in mind that time is an illusion and does not exist in the spirit world; therefore, it is not always easy or possible for a medium or psychic to give exact dates or times within the messages he or she conveys. Also, not everything is literal or to be taken as fact, so a spirit's message can be misinterpreted.

When you get something wrong in a reading, try to go back to the information and reinterpret it. Sometimes this will provide the right information. Sometimes you will have been spot on in the first place, and the client just didn't realize it. If this happens, the information may click for the client later. Sometimes your mind will add in incorrect information as it tries to help. I find that when I get something wrong, it is best to let it go and move on to the next bit of information a spirit wishes me to pass on.

Always be grateful for any information you receive. It is a great honour to help people and spirits connect, to give someone guidance, and to help someone to understand his or her life better. People place their trust in the information you pass on, so you have a responsibility to always give the best messages that you can when doing a reading. Some psychics tell clients negative things that upset them or frighten them, and they leave the reading stressed and worried. I've done thousands of readings, but I've never told people things that would upset them, as I believe that when people have a reading done, they should leave feeling good about themselves and happy about the information that they received.

The power of suggestion can be a powerful thing, so just suggesting that something bad may happen can really affect a person negatively. As a psychic, you should always be careful about what you tell people and how you tell it. You don't need to withhold information, as there are ways of saying something negative without being cruel or blunt. I always try to come from a place of compassion and speak with a kind heart in a gentle way so that clients are aware of potentially negative information but are not upset or scared by what I tell them. I try to respect their feelings, I can misinterpret messages, so I point out that there are many possible outcomes and give the information as just a possibility.

A psychic shouldn't be arrogant and think that everything he or she picks up is 100 per cent accurate. No psychic is always correct during a reading, as information can be misinterpreted or off the mark in many ways. When you perform a reading, only accept the information that feels right for you and let go of anything that doesn't feel right.

Another important tip is to protect your energy field so that you don't take on negative energy. Working with other energies can drain your own energy level, so it's important to cleanse and protect yourself and your personal energy fields. There are many ways to do this. Having the intention to do so is a good start, and then believe in your own ability to do this, for if you don't believe, it won't work. This applies to most things that deal with energy. You can see some methods of protection earlier in the last chapter in the section "Psychic Protection."

Spirits, guides, and angels are around us all the time, and they're usually good, but as with all things in the universe, where there is light there is also dark, so it's possible to pick up on negative or unwanted spirits. I always ask for only the good and try to repel or reflect the negative. If I do pick up a negative spirit, I ask it to leave and tell it that I don't want it to hang around me. I then ring a bell, burn some sage, and send it on its way with love, which is important, as sending it any negative energy will only add to its negativity. When you send it love and positive energy, you help the spirit become more positive.

The best way for you to develop your abilities is to practise using them regularly. It is best to practise with people you don't know very well, so then you won't have prior knowledge about that person that could interfere with what you pick up.

Although all of your psychic senses can be utilized to pick up information, clairvoyance and clairaudience are the two main ones to use, as these allow you to receive detailed information.

You can practise developing these abilities through meditation alone. The longer you can still your mind during meditation, the more open it will be to receiving information. The more you practise visualization, the more open your mind will become to receiving mental images, and the more you have conversations in meditation, the more open you will be to hearing voices in your mind. Every time you meditate, you develop your psychic senses and abilities and allow your mind to become more used to perceiving with your psychic senses.

All of the information you receive will come to you through your psychic senses, so pay attention to your thoughts, notice everything you see and hear and feel both physically and emotionally. Usually the first thought that comes to you is right, so try not to second-guess yourself. I like to keep a pen and paper with me so I can write down information whenever it comes through.

Try this little exercise at home to practice using your senses: When your telephone rings, before you answer it, take a deep breath, focus, and ask yourself these questions. Is the caller male or female? Is it someone I know or a stranger? What is the call about? Make a note of the number of times you are correct and incorrect. Do this over the course of a week or two, and you'll notice that the more you do it, the more accurate you become.

Psychometry: Readings Through Touch.

Our bodies are continually giving off energy and absorbing it from the environment. The body is an amazing mechanism. It gives off sound, light, heat, electricity, magnetism, electromagnetism, and other energies, and it can also respond to all of these energies. The subconscious mind monitors and mediates all of this interaction. We leave behind the energy we put out, and the longer we have contact with a place or thing, the more energy we leave on it, where it remains long after we are gone. When our energy fields come into contact with other energy fields left behind by others, the fields interact and communicate. By controlling your subconscious mind, you can access these energies and the information they carry.

All of the information you receive from energy comes in through your psychic senses. You must train your mind to be observant of the subtle information you perceive with your physical senses, in order to receive information with your psychic senses. Look for anything that comes, such as thoughts that randomly pop into your head, sounds you think you hear, discomfort in part of the body or tingling, any sensation or feeling. You can do this by asking questions: What is the general tone or mood of the energies you've encountered? How do they make you feel? What are your physical senses telling you? Have any thoughts popped into your mind? When you focus on an object, person, or place, what do you pick up? How are you connecting to the energy of that object, person, or place?

Note, too, that it's possible to connect to the energy of things and people from great distances away, but that comes with practice. When starting out working with energies to get information, it is best to make a physical connection so that your own energy can interact with the energies you are connecting to. This way, you more easily get more information.

This is what psychometry is all about. It is the connection of your energy field to the energy field of a place, object, or person outside yourself in order to receive information through the psychic senses.

One of the hardest parts of psychometry is understanding the information that comes in and interpreting it accurately.

Sometimes your conscious mind will jump to a conclusion about what you've received and will give you the wrong interpretation of it. When something like this happens, just let it go and refocus on the information you are receiving. Make note of the information, even if it doesn't make sense, and continue until there is no more information coming and you keep drawing a blank. The more you practice this the more information you will receive and the better you will understand it.

Psychic Tools

As you develop your psychic abilities, you may wish to add tools to support your abilities. Many divination tools, including tarot cards, palm reading, runes, and pendulums, can be helpful, as many of them allow you to get detailed information for someone you're reading for without relying on your psychic senses. Therefore, if you learn to use one or more of these tools, you can always fall back on them if you find you're not picking up a lot of information with your psychic senses. All you need to do to learn to use any of these is to study and memorize the information about it. You can then put it into action and get amazing results. You can practise using them on anyone who's willing, and when you feel you're skilled enough, you can start charging money for your services. Divination tools can be a lot of fun to use and are surprisingly accurate.

Tarot Cards

Tarot cards have been used for centuries all over the world, and they can be used without any psychic abilities. You just need to learn about each card's meaning and how its position in a spread and its combination with other cards affect that meaning. It's helpful to memorize as much of this information as you can so that you don't need to continually refer to a guide during a reading. To learn how to use tarot cards, you can take a course or study from a book at home.

When tarot cards are used, the energy of the person having the reading connects to the energy of the cards and causes the cards to fall in an order when they're shuffled to give the specific cards and layout when dealt. The cards and the spread they're dealt in then provides general information about the person having the reading and his or her life. The client may be able to relate this general information to something specific in their life.

When a tarot reader incorporates his or her psychic abilities and information he or she receives through the psychic senses into a reading, the more meaning and understanding the client will receive from the reading.

You can also ask the cards questions and deal spreads to get the answer. By putting the right intention and positive thought into your energy, you increase the possibilities that the spread will provide more accurate information.

When you're not using your cards, it helps to place a clear quartz crystal on the pack to neutralize their energy and clear away the energies others have left on them so the cards can absorb new energies the next time they're used. Wrapping the cards with a silk or satin cloth has a similar effect.

There are many different styles of tarot cards available and many other types of divining cards. You can use whichever cards you wish to use as long as you're comfortable with them and know their meanings. You can purchase many different kinds of guidance cards, including those with angel cards and animal guides. Some give more detailed meaning than others, but with any pack, you need to get to know your cards well before you can do readings with them.

Palm Reading

Palm reading is another tool one can explore using that doesn't require the use of psychic abilities. The palms of our hands contain all the information about our lives. Everyone's hands are unique in shape and size and in the lines and other markings on them. When you study palmistry, you'll learn about what variations in these shapes, lines, and markings can tell you in general and specifically about many different aspects of a person's life, including general personality characteristics and health, marriages, and children.

I recommend reading a few books on palmistry to learn about what all the variations in the lines and shapes mean. It can take a while to take in all this information, but once you know it, you'll be able to tell people many things about themselves just from their palms. It is handy to keep a small torch and a magnify glass for seeing the finer lines on the hand.

There is some question about which hand to read, the right hand is said to show your destiny, as you create your life to be, and the left is said to show your fate as God intended it. Many believe you should read from the dominant hand, however, there are many other interpretations, all of which have merit. It is up to you as an individual to choose what feels right for you. I like to read the dominant hand, but will sometimes look at both.

Overview

There is much to be said about tools and methods of using the psychic abilities, including healing, fortune telling, personality profiling with numbers or astrological charts, communication with other life forms, and communication with mystic forces from all civilizations and societies from the beginning of life on this planet. All of these many fields of what is now considered New Age practice and philosophy have always been with us, and more and more people believe that these have merit, are credible, and aren't evil or wrong or bad. Those of us who use them simply offer our services to help others in whichever way we can, the best we can.

I encourage you to experiment with New Age services, which now also include reiki treatments, crystal healings, ThetaHealing, aromatherapy, naturopathy, herbalism, sound healing, and any number of other therapies that can be very beneficial for your health. As Psychics, mediums, and other seers can tell you about your past, present, and future and can communicate with spirits and pass on these messages to you, they offer many benefits to their clients. Many courses and so much information about each type of service, tradition, and belief system is easily accessible to those who wish to learn about them. The more we learn and use these techniques, the more we see the truth that lies within, and the more benefits we gain on our journey of life.

Chapter 8

Shows and Readings

Since I started reading professionally in 2002, I've done thousands of readings for people both privately and at shows. I'm predominately a spirit medium, meaning that I connect with spirits and pass on messages to their loved ones in our realm, but I am also a psychic, which means that I can also pick up information from the past, present, and future about a person I'm reading for. Often I amaze myself as well as my clients with the details I pass on in the readings I do.

When I do readings, I prefer to hold the client's hand so that we have a physical connection, but this is not always possible, and a good reading does not depend on this. So, in addition to face-to-face readings, I can do phone and Skype readings, and I have done them for people all over the world. Although I am only connecting to clients' voices, and I am still able to bring through accurate, detailed messages for them regardless of distance. I enjoy my mediumship work the best, as I find it the most rewarding part of doing readings; however, not everyone has a lot of spirits connected to them or even wants to hear messages from spirit. In these cases, I just use my psychic abilities, to add depth to a reading, I read palms and tarot cards. I normally use these tools near the end of a reading, depending on how much information is coming through from spirit.

I am still able to do a tarot card spread over the phone or Skype, but palm readings can only be done when you see me in person. Some people like having these done, but other people prefer to focus on messages from spirit. This is a personal choice depending on what you hope to gain from your reading. Tarot cards can be very accurate, and when combined with my psychic abilities, they can help me better understand issues you've been through or that are about to happen in your life. Palm readings can tell me a lot about the type of person you are and many of your characteristics in addition to what has passed and what is yet to come in your life, so this is also a helpful psychic tool. There are many other psychic tools, and all have merit, but it is the person doing the reading that makes all of the difference. So, when you're looking to have a reading done, it's important to find someone you connect with and that you've heard good feedback about.

I've had quite a lot of psychic readings done for me over the years. When another psychic does a reading for me, I'm always open and hope it will be good. I'm happy to be told anything, and I look for things that I can relate to about myself or my family; my past, present, or future; or any messages that come from spirit. I always hope for at least some information that's specific and verifiable to some degree. Unfortunately, I'm often disappointed, as the information is very vague, is completely wrong, or just does not fit.

I have had some good readings and some okay readings, but up to one third of the readings I've received have been a waste of my time and money. Perhaps this is because I compare what I receive in a reading with what I give in the readings I do. I never complain or say bad things about a psychic who does a bad reading, but I also won't recommend him or her to anyone. I realize that psychics have bad days and times in which they have trouble connecting, it may just be that our energies were different. I only ever recommend psychics whose readings have made me happy, but I feel it is up to each individual to choose who does his or her reading.

From my experience, I'd estimate that about 20 per cent of the psychics out there are not that good and should not be charging for what they offer, as they give nothing specific or verifiable; up to 40 per cent of psychics are just okay, as they get some relevant information that a client can connect with; and maybe 30 per cent are good and give some specific detail and a lot of information a client can relate to. The other 10 per cent are really good. They give a lot of specific detail, and clients can relate to most of what they say. Having said this, not every reading is the same, and depending on the connection a psychic makes with a client, any psychic could fall into any of the above groups.

Of the readings I've done, I would say that most of my clients would put me in the top 10 per cent, or say that I'm exceptionally good at doing readings. Maybe 30 per cent would just say I'm in the 30 per cent bracket (good), and possibly 5 per cent would put me down as just okay. Perhaps for every 1 in every couple of thousand readings, I may even fall into the lowest bracket and the client felt I was hopeless. No one is great at every single reading, and no one can honestly claim to be 100 per cent accurate about everything they pick up on.

My readings normally last about an hour, but some are longer. I specialize as a medium, so I bring through varied messages from spirit, often with names and specific details about the deceased.

I also pick up on information related to the past, present, and future, and some of this information may be a little vague, but I also bring through a lot of specific information that the client can relate to. I am always receiving feedback about my predictions of the future eventuating. I also do a tarot spread to bring through more information, and then, if there's still time, I'll read a client's palm and pick up a lot more information.

Some readings start out slowly, and I get a few things wrong, but once I make a connection with the information, it usually flows. I may ask for confirmation on the information I receive, but I don't like a client to tell me too much. My clients mostly walk away with a lot of specific information. I can honestly say that at least 80 per cent of the information I give is accurate. Some people have been hard to read for, but I've almost always still brought through some specific information for them that they can relate to. Even with the readings that I've felt weren't as good as usual, my clients have been happy.

I set high standards for myself and always give the best I can. I use a lot of compassion and love and often give advice. I try not to bring my ego into a reading, as I know I'm merely a messenger. Doing this work requires a lot of concentration and can be very draining, but it's also very rewarding.

When I connect to spirit, information can come in from any of my psychic senses. Some spirits are easier to connect with than others.

Whether you're having a psychic reading for the first time or you've seen other psychics or myself before, here are some tips to get the most out of your reading:

Relax! Tension or unease can block messages from mediums and psychics, so take a few deep breaths and let go of your tension before the reading begins.

Let go of your expectations. When we have specific things that we want to hear, we can ignore what's being said to us and miss important details. It's okay to want to hear from someone or to want to hear something specific, but let go of the need for this and just allow your energy to be open to receive whatever comes in. I've found over the years that when people want something really badly, such as to get back with their ex or to have a baby, they can become obsessive, and this affects their energy fields and distorts the information that I pick up on. If you go into a reading with an obsession, then the psychic may pick up on this information and misinterpret it as your future energy instead of its being your strong desire, so always try to let go of specific needs or expectations before your reading. It's okay to ask questions, but realize that a psychic won't always be able to answer them.

Be open-minded. Whatever your beliefs before the reading, it's important to let go of any preconceived notions, be open-minded, and be willing to accept that not everything can be explained and that there's nothing wrong or evil about having a psychic reading.

If for any reason you're not happy with your reading, it's best to let the psychic know. If I feel I haven't picked up much information for a client, I may decide not to charge for the time; however, if I feel I have given a lot of information, then I may still ask an unhappy client to pay part of or the whole fee for the reading. Each psychic or medium has his or her own policy on this. You can always refuse to pay if you're unhappy, but if the psychic insists, then it's better to just pay and take the lesson.

Remember, too, that the power of word of mouth is very strong, so tell others if your experience was good or bad, as your review will help others to find good psychics and avoid the ones that aren't as good.

Being a medium is a very rewarding job. Often clients come to me who are grieving after the loss of a loved one, and being able to connect them with those loved ones brings them a lot of comfort. Readings can be very emotional for clients, even strong, tough men, and many people cry when they hear information from their loved ones from the other side. Many times these are tears of joy. Clients almost always leave a reading feeling happy and with a sense that they've renewed the connection with those they've lost. Many sceptics walk away with new beliefs and more open minds as they struggle to understand how I knew all of that information about them.

In almost all of my readings I bring through information about my clients' past and describe things to them that no one else knows but them. These may be about events in their lives or their loved ones' lives. I've described how people passed away and even what they were buried in, and I've picked up on their memories and described things from their lives that they've related to. I've also been known to describe people's homes without ever seeing them, even objects inside. It can feel like I'm walking through their home and seeing everything there. Often I'm led to those things which have a sentimental value to a client.

At one of my shows, I had picked up on a spirit connected to a lady, and after describing a few things about the spirit to her, I suddenly picked up "pancakes." I had no idea what this meant or what it related to, but when I mentioned it to the lady, she immediately burst into tears. I had no idea why, and I asked her how that related to her. She told me that the woman in spirit I had connected to had been the lady's best friend and had passed away two years before. Every year, on the lady's birthday, she and her friend got together for pancakes. The friend sprinkled hundreds and thousands on the pancakes and lit a birthday candle. So, when I mentioned the pancakes, this lady knew for sure that her friend was there passing on messages to me.

During readings I'll pick up on names of people in spirit and will know if the spirit is a family member or friend, but sometimes this information isn't clear. I may get a name that sounds similar to the correct name, or I may just get the first initial. Other times I may not be given the name at all and will only pick up on other information for the client to recognize. This can be a bit tricky and confusing, so it's helpful to get a little feedback on the information I'm passing on. Simple yes and no answers aren't always the best, as a little more feedback can mean the difference between my going more deeply, looking for specific detail or letting that piece of a message go and moving on to other messages. When I was close to the mark on something, clients have just said no and told me nothing to say that I was near the heart of a matter, so I let it go. Then, at the end of the reading, when they've asked me to pick up on something specific, I've realized that this was what I was getting before but simply hadn't been specific enough for the client.

Some psychics and mediums will hold on to a piece of information until they get confirmation about it, to the point that they become dogmatic and will keep pushing the client to connect with the information, like the mediums are convinced that they've been given the information for a reason and aren't willing to accept that they could be wrong. I don't do this. If the client doesn't connect to something I pick up on, I simply let it go and move on. Often other information comes through that the client does connect to and ties in to the information I had previously, or they'll remember later what the first piece of information related to or will talk to someone else who can relate to that information. Of course, there are also times when I've simply been wrong.

Some people can put up walls that make it harder for me to do readings for them. They may be open to what I can do and believe in my abilities but try to test me or expect me to get very specific things straight away at the start of the reading. Sometimes I will blow a client away from the start, but more often, a reading starts out slowly, and the information can be slightly off the mark. Then, as I get more information both from spirit and the client, I'm able to piece things together and then make a stronger connection, and that's when the information flows more fluidly, and I can pass on more specific details.

In any reading, my goal is to help people, and I feel I do this more often than not. I often see myself as a counsellor or therapist, as I'm able to help them cope with grief or give them hope for a brighter future. I am not here to make anyone believe one thing or another; all people are different and choose their own beliefs. People will believe what they want to believe, and there is nothing I can say or do to change them. The only way a sceptic will become a believer is if he or she has an experience that persuades him or her to believe.

I've met many sceptics in my line of work, but most of those who have readings with me walk out believing, as I've brought through information for them that I couldn't know unless I communicated with spirit. I've even brought through spirits that had been sceptics when they were alive. Most times, if sceptics can't explain or rationalize what they experience, they'll begin to

Suzie Price

accept psychic phenomenon as real or at least be more open to the possibility that it's real.

Still, some people have thought that I did a lot of research to find out the information I gave them. They've asked me if I looked up information on Facebook or talked to their family or friends about it. Some people have said, "I don't know how you know all of these things but I am still not convinced." People can become so set in their thinking that they simply cannot accept psychic abilities as real. Luckily, I don't come across too many of these people.

In general, I believe people are becoming more aware and more accepting of psychic abilities, as more and more people are opening their minds. Psychics and mediums are no longer ridiculed as we once were, and we're seen as evil less often. Eventually, the sceptics will open their minds and change their opinions. We only have to keep doing what we do and touch more people to open their minds.

Whether I do personal readings or readings at shows, I'm always nervous and anxious before I start. I worry that the people won't be happy with what I pick up or that I won't make a good connection that satisfies them. I especially worry that they'll get angry at me, although this has only ever happened to me a few times in the many years I've used my abilities. One instance happened when I did a phone reading for a young man from New Zealand. I started the reading but didn't tell him something he could connect to straight away, and within a minute, he yelled and swore at me and put me down, which really upset me. Another person got up halfway through the reading, stated that she wasn't happy with the reading, and left. In a few cases, I've felt that clients weren't happy with what I was picking up for them, early in the reading and when they confirmed this, we decided to stop the reading then. A couple of people have told me that they were dissatisfied at the end of their readings. I waived my fee each time this happened, but a couple of these people still seemed quite angry and aggressive. I never handle aggression well, and their responses have made me cry. Whenever any client isn't satisfied, it shatters my confidence, and there have been times when I've felt so bad that I wanted to stop doing readings completely, but Stephen has helped me work through this and pushed me to do the next reading, and I have gone great. Stephen likes to quote me the old saying; "You can please some of the people all of the time and all of the people some of the time, but you can't please all of the people all of the time!" Thankfully I only get one or two of these types of readings each year.

Interestingly, the lady who walked out on me in the middle of her reading came back to see me about three years later. She had recently lost someone close to her, and her friend had urged her to come and give me another chance. I didn't recognize her. This time, she was much more open, and after I had finished her reading, she said I had blown her away with the information I brought through, and she told me that she had been to see me a few years before and had walked out halfway through her previous reading. This was the only time that had happened, so I remembered her and thanked her for coming back. She was so happy that she had.

Every time I connect with spirit for people, the spirits send love. I often feel their emotions and other sensations as if they were my own. It can be like I become the spirits or the spirits become part of me as I connect to their personalities and get insights into their lives. I can feel pain or discomfort in areas of my body that may relate to how the spirits passed or to ailments they had when they were alive. Luckily, this is mostly a glimpse into the pain and doesn't last long. All in all, this is a pleasant experience and I enjoy being able to do it.

Because I do so many readings, I usually don't remember much about them, but every now and then, I'll do a reading that sticks in my memory. I would like to share some of these memories.

At a show, I connected with a lady's late brother. I picked up his name and a few identifying details, and then I described that he had committed suicide by hanging himself in the shed and said that this woman had found his body the next day. After picking up a few more details from him, another spirit come through who told me that he was this woman's father. He told me that he had died the same way as his son about eighteen months after his son committed suicide, and this woman had also found his body. He gave me a lot of other details about himself and his life, all of which the woman confirmed. Then a third spirit, a woman, came through. She told me her name and that she was this woman's sister. I was shown details of her passing, and I passed them on. "She was killed in a car accident," I said. "She was driving up a hill not kept far enough to the left when another car came over the hill and hit her head-on. She died almost instantly." But then the spirit told me that her three year old daughter was asleep on the back seat at the time of the accident and was thrown through the windscreen on impact, landing in the bushes nearby. The police and paramedics didn't find her until almost three hours later. She didn't die in the accident but was in a coma for three months afterwards. The woman confirmed that everything that I had picked up was spot on, and I felt so sad for that she had had to go through all of this and lose so much of her family. The woman was overwhelmed by everything I had picked up on, but she was grateful that I was able to pass on messages from her late family members.

At another show, I connected with a beautiful woman from an island somewhere in the Pacific. A young man came through for her in spirit, related to me his name, and said that he had passed away in a motorbike accident. He had been travelling too fast on a coastal road and lost control of his bike. The lady confirmed everything I said, and then the man told me to say, "This happened on the Cook Islands." The lady was blown away and asked how I knew that. "Well, he told me," I said. "He's standing beside you."

I went on to describe how this woman and her brother had been great mates, and I pointed out that she was wearing a friendship ring that he had given her. He wanted her to know that he loved her and was with her always and that he was okay with her moving to Australia, as he said that she would be happier here.

I often pick up details about how a spirit passed away, and this can be quite unpleasant, especially in cases of accidents. In one reading, the client's nephew came through and told me he had passed away just three months before and that he was only fifteen. I was shown that he was at his home with his friends and had gotten out his father's shotgun to play with. When he was putting the gun back into the cupboard, it went off and shot him in the stomach. I saw an image of him lying on the lounge with his mother, who held him and cried as they waited for an ambulance, but he passed away before it arrived. I felt very emotional as I witnessed this, and the image has stuck in my head because the scene was so emotionally intense.

I always ask spirits not to show me anything too graphic, and they mostly honour my request. Despite this, I can still be emotionally affected by the things they show me, especially when the spirits were children when they passed over.

I did a reading at a show for a man in his mid to late twenties. When I held his hand, a toddler come through who had passed away about two years before, it was his son. I was given the boy's name and told that his father had broken up with his mother when he was still a baby. Then, this child told me that he had been beaten to death by his mother's new partner, but the police couldn't prove it, and no charges had been laid. The man confirmed all of this and everything else I told him. This was a very emotional reading for both the man and me.

I often bring through messages for people whose loved one has committed suicide, and the people left behind are often worried that the spirit of their loved one may be trapped or in turmoil because of this. I have never connected to such a spirit that has indicated he or she is anything other than at peace. They always tell me to pass on the fact that they are very sorry for causing their deaths and so much heartache for their family and friends.

When clients don't connect to the information I bring through, I end up feeling frustrated with spirit and myself. One instance of this happened when I was doing readings for a hen night. During the first reading, a spirit came through for the client, but she couldn't connect to it. The spirit was a lady, I kept getting she was small, but I didn't get a name, so I said to the client, "this spirit is a lady and she saying she was a small lady or little? The client said, "No, I don't know anyone that was little." I moved on from this and tried to pick up other information, and a few things I said did make sense to this young lady, but she said no to most of it. After a few minutes, I told her that I wasn't picking up much, and I let her sit down with her friends again and I brought another guest of the party up.

The next reading went well, as I picked up lots of things that the client connected to, and then the next reading also went well. The accuracy of these two readings opened the minds of the other guests, including the first lady. A spirit came through and gave me a name, and the first lady put her hand up to say that she had a close friend with that name who had passed. I got the lady to come back up the front and again, and I got that this spirit was a small or little lady, and told this to the girl again. She said that her friend wasn't little; but her last name was Small! I continued the reading, and I ended up passing on a lot of information for her. This just shows how information may be slightly off the mark and that you need to have an open mind to see how information may relate or connect to a client. Don't discard anything you're told, as there is almost always some connection if you properly join the dots to create a clearer picture.

When people are open and believe in what I do, they can connect to most of the information easily, but those who have doubts can block the information or simply not make meaningful connections because of their doubts.

At the same hen party, the host told me that her mother had taken a shot at her about getting a psychic to do readings at the party, as her mother thought the idea of psychics was all crap, and she stayed in the kitchen for most of the party, although she could still see and hear everything. About ninety minutes into my two-hour session, spirit gave me a name, and I asked if anyone knew someone alive or dead with this name. The girls all pointed to the mother in the kitchen and said that that was her name. I asked her to come out and sit with me for a minute, and very reluctantly, she sat beside me and held my hand.

I asked her if her mother had passed, and she said yes. I then asked if her mother had lived with her for a couple of years just before she passed away, and again the woman said yes. I then received her mother's name and was told that was correct too. I then asked the woman if she had a pool in the back yard, and she said yes to this too. Then I said that there was like an entertainment room at the back of the house near the pool with big sliding glass doors. Again, the woman confirmed this, so I described the room as having a pool table, a bar, and a dart board in it. Again, yes. I then said that this room connected to a lounge room. Yes. The lounge room had a big glass cabinet. Yes. There was a picture of this woman and her mum on top of the cabinet in a picture frame with flowers on it.

"How do you know all of this?" the woman said. "Have you been to my house before?"

Of course, I said, "No. Your mother told me."

This woman was just stunned. I sat with her for another ten minutes and brought through a lot of information from her late mother. After the reading, she knew that there was much more to the spirit world then she had thought, and she apologized to her daughter for having a shot at her about getting a psychic for her party.

Some people are so stuck in their beliefs that their inflexible, and this creates impenetrable barriers for them and for me. I once did for a mother and daughter, and the mother also invited her sister to sit in. The aunty was very negative and tried to rationalize everything I said, saying things like, "Well that could apply to many people." A lot of what I picked up didn't connect for them, and the aunty's negative energy really affected the reading. At the end of the reading, I didn't want to charge them, but the daughter insisted on paying me.

I thought about the reading all the way home, and when I got back, I called the daughter and offered to do another reading for her and her mother together without her aunty. She agreed that her aunty's attitude might have affected the reading and said that she was happy to come to me for another reading. I found some room to fit them in two weeks later, and the mother and daughter came to my house for another reading. This time. I was able to make a much better connection to spirit, and they had a great reading. They left with pages of information, and they were so happy.

When people have specific expectations about what they want to hear, this can also create blockages. A lady who had lost her daughter came to me for a reading, and when she arrived, I made a great connection for her, and a lot of specific information came through, but at the end of the reading, the lady looked sad and disappointed. I asked her if she was happy with the reading, and she said she was, but, "If my daughter was here, then why didn't she show herself to me?" She had heard that spirits can show themselves to people if they want to, and she was hoping that I could facilitate this and allow her to see her daughter one last time. I tried to explain to her that that can happen but that she would need to do a lot of work on herself to facilitate that. Making such a connection required a lot of concentration, so she would need to focus her own energy to a point that made this possible, and even then, she still may not be able to see her daughter in the way that she had hoped to, as a sighting of a spirit was more often a quick flash that left an impressions on the mind than like seeing and talking to a real person. I spent another thirty minutes trying to explain how it worked, but I could tell she just couldn't get her head around it all. She was too lost in her grief and too stuck on having a last goodbye with her daughter like in the movies.

When I do readings, I start by seeing what I can pick up and which spirits are around that want to connect with clients. After I've done this, I always ask clients if there is anything else they want to know about or anyone else that they want to hear from. Most of the time people will tell me if they do, but some people seem to want to test me, and they say nothing, as they think that I should know because I'm a psychic.

This happened with a lady at a show. She seemed to want to test me through the whole reading. She gave me very little feedback, only answering with a yes or a no, and when I was close to the mark, she only said, "No, but you're close." Her son was with her at the show, and her late husband came through. I told the lady that I was getting something about renovations and that I felt they were at her son's house. She told me no but that I was close, so I kept trying to figure out what the message meant. Eventually I said, "Painting," and she said, "Yes. My son has been painting some of the rooms inside the house." I also picked up that her late husband's car was silver and that he took a lot of pride in it, washing it and cleaning all the time. She said yes and then asked me if I could tell her what kind of car it was. I told her it was some type of sports car, and she said it was but wanted me to tell her what type of car it was. I said, "Some kind of big cat," but she wanted to know what kind of cat. I wasn't up on cars and didn't know much about different models, and although I kept trying. I couldn't get anything more than the information about the cat. She kept pushing me to see if I could get it. I ended up saying I was sorry but I couldn't get it, and finally she told me that it was a Jaguar. Right throughout the reading, she made it as hard as she could for me and didn't elaborate on anything until I exactly hit the mark.

I almost never do any reading without them asking me to first, or, at a show, I'll ask them if it's okay if I tell them something I've picked up, but occasionally I haven't done this. One day, I was down at the shopping centre when I saw two young men approaching me with pamphlets in their hands. I knew that they were about to sell me something. They said hi and asked if I could spare a minute, but before they could continue, I looked at one of the young men and said, "Hi. You play musical instruments, don't you?" He looked shocked, and I said, "You can play about five different instruments. You're very talented."

He said, "Yes, but how do you know that? We haven't met before, have we?"

I told him, "No, we haven't met. I'm a psychic medium, and as soon as I seen you, I had a flash of you playing all of these different instruments."

Both this man and his partner were astonished. I ended up talking to them for a few minutes. I picked up a few things about the other young man, too. They totally forgot to tell me about what was on the pamphlets, and I told them it was lovely talking to them and then just went on walking.

I love doing readings and find it very rewarding that I can help so many people in so many ways. I remember one lady in her early twenties contacted me, told me her name was Stacy, and asked for my help because she felt she had a bad spirit attached to her. She said that she heard a voice in her head that was very negative. She saw counsellors and had been to many doctors. She harmed herself and had tried to take her own life a few times. She was on a pension and had no car or money, but I agreed to help her. Stephen drove me to her flat in Newcastle, which she shared with some friends. Stacy was there with her flatmates when we arrived. She was very thin and drawn and did not look well. I sat and talked with her while Stephen cleansed the apartment using sage and bells. I picked up on an old negative spirit with Stacy, and this spirit told me that when Stacy was about six years old, her parents had taken her with them when they did an exorcism, and the spirit had left that person but had attached to Stacy.

Stacy told me that she had felt funny and not right since then. There were times when she felt she had no control over her actions and that she had encountered problems in many areas of her life that just seemed to get worse. She then started self-harming as a teenager. Her parents took her to doctors and therapists, but nobody understood what she was going through. When she was sixteen, she left home and lived on the streets for six months before finding help through some friends. She had tried to kill herself three times, twice by cutting her wrists and once by overdosing. She had heard this voice in her head as long as she could remember, and it scared her.

I had her sit on a chair in the middle of the room, and I started by having Stephen to do a cleansing with the bells and sage around her. Then I stood behind her and called in light and love and my guides and angels and God, and I asked the spirit to leave. I repeated this several times, and then Stephen and I both did an energy healing on Stacy for another thirty minutes.

After this, Stacy said she felt completely different. She described the sensations she felt during the process and said she now felt lighter and more positive. Stephen talked with her about the law of attraction and gave her some tips about how she could improve her life, and then we wished her the best and told her to not hesitate to contact us again if she needed us. The whole process had taken about two hours, and we felt we had done all we could to help her.

Three years later, Stacy sent me a friend request on Facebook and included a lovely message. Her life had completely changed after she had seen me. The voices had gone, and she had gotten her life together. She had been in a relationship for the past two years and had a beautiful baby boy who was ten months old. In the pictures on her page, she looked much healthier. She had colour in her skin and meat on her bones. She looked radiant and happy. She was so full of gratitude, and I was thankful that I had been able to help.

These are just a few examples of the work I do every day. The vast majority of people who've had readings with me are very happy, and many return for more readings. I also help people in many other ways. I have talked to dozens of children with psychic abilities at the request of their parents to explain what they're experiencing. I'm often asked to clear negative spirits from people's homes and workplaces. I also teach psychic-development and spiritual-awareness courses, and I'm often asked for advice on many types of problems. Then there is my work with Haunted Australia, my shows, and the interviews I do on radio and television. Of all my work, my real passion is my mediumship. I love doing readings for people and opening their minds and their beliefs. I love being able to connect people to their loved ones and to bring them the comfort of knowing that their loved ones are never far away and are watching out for them. So many people I have done readings for describe the experience as life changing! I find this so rewarding. Doing readings can be draining and tiring, not to mention stressful and scary, but knowing I have made a positive difference for someone makes it all worth it. I feel so blessed to do this type of work, and I wouldn't change that for any reason.

Chapter 9

Questions and Answers

People often ask me questions or want my advice on things, sometimes when what they really want is a short reading. People are always curious about the future or about their loved ones who have passed.

When I'm out and about, people recognize me and know what I do, and they often ask questions like, "What do you see for me?" I always respond politely, sometimes chatting and even giving them what I pick up at the time if I have time and am not too tired or focused on other things. But if I'm busy or unwell or need some downtime, I'll quickly explain that I'm not able to take the time for a reading right now and will give my reasons.

People have also tried to take advantage of me in the past, always wanting information, and this is when I need to ask myself whether the friendship is worth it, if it feels like it drains me. I try to explain as gently as I can without being rude that I can't give them information, but some people just refuse to take hints or listen to anything that does not suit them. These seemingly simple requests also come to me through emails or messages on Facebook.

I am always happy to give advice when I am able to, but I don't like being pressured to do free readings. I have gained from all of my experiences, and I know that what I give out comes back to me, so if I'm able to give, I do, but we all must set boundaries and be true to ourselves. Talking to people and giving a little something can lead to more business, it can push me and test me to make me grow, but I must choose what I do at any given time.

Some people think that just because I'm psychic, I know everything, and this is a common joke I get from people who don't understand much about psychic abilities. I can assure you that this is not the case. Although I may pick up some things wherever I am, I don't have my abilities turned on 24/7, and even if I did, I don't receive answers to everything.

The answers to many questions that people commonly ask me have already been explained in my book, such as those about psychic protection and where spirits go once they've passed. In this section, I've shared some other common questions so that I can answer them for more curious people.

This first question is one of my favourites. People who ask this are often scratching their heads trying to reason it out. The conversation normally goes like this:

Q. How do you know this stuff?
A. I'm a medium and I'm psychic, and I just pass on what I pick up.

Q. But how do you do that?
A. I just allow myself to be open to the information, and I pay attention to what I receive. The information comes to me in many different ways.

Q. But where does this information come from?

A. From spirits who are connected to you or from my spirit guides.

Q. So is it real? Like, are there really spirits there?

A. Yes, it is real. There are spirits, spirit guides, and angels. They are always around us, and it is possible to communicate with them.

Q. Really?

A. Yes really. They do exist and it is real.

Q. So do they actually talk to you?

A. Sometimes, but the information usually comes in through my psychic senses and I have to work out what it means.

I love the look on people's faces when they have trouble getting their heads around this. I know that they'll think differently after this, as once the mind is open, it can't go back to the way it was before.

Q. I always seem to attract the wrong type of man into my life. I'm currently single again and want to find the right person. Is this possible?

A. Yes, this is possible, but you'll need to put out the right kind of energy to attract the right person. To do this, you need to take a closer look at what you're putting out and make some changes within yourself to put out a different energy. It often helps to write things down so you can have a good look at where you've been, where you are now, and where you want to be.

Start by writing down some things about your past relationships on two separate pages or in two notebooks, one for the negative things and one for positive things. Write all that was bad and all that was good. Then, do the same thing for your present life. Once you have these lists, read them carefully, and make sure you haven't left anything out and that everything is honest and true for you.

Now, write out one more page, only this time, write down all of the good things you would like to see in your life. Go into as much detail as you can to put out to the universe exactly what you would like in a partner, in your relationship, and in your life. Take a look at your finished list and ask yourself what changes you need to make within yourself to obtain this life and this relationship. Then, be the person you wish to become. When you put that energy out, the right people and circumstances will be attracted to you. They may take a little time to materialize, but if you put out the intention and focus on the outcome, then they will come to you.

Q: What kind of experiences have you had with spirits over the years? Are you ever scared?

A: I've had many experiences with spirits, including those in which otherwise unexplainable things have happened to me. I often see spirits and can talk with them, I've seen lights flickering, light globes exploding, things falling as if they have been pushed, objects flying off shelves or jumping into the air, and doors opening, closing, and even locking on their own. When I ask for signs, the signs turn up soon after. I often feel spirits touch me on the shoulder or the back, and I'll get goosebumps or cold shivers. A spirit even held me down in bed once, which was not very pleasant and frightened me. I also woke one night to see my bedroom full of ghouls, which are grey spirits with no facial features. They were scary, and I quickly got up and saged my room to clear them away.

However, I've had mostly pleasant experiences with spirits for as long as I can remember. Not every spirit is nice, and I know that there are darker, heavier spirits out there, but they've mostly stayed out of my life.

Q: I need help with a former boyfriend who died in '07 in a drink-driving accident. He has since told me he was sorry for cheating on me, and I forgave him, but I feel I shouldn't have. Is it true that spirits say they love you then cheat on you when they are dead too? I feel he's cheating on me now. I'm still angry at him. He even told me he would wait for me on the other side, and I told him not to, but he doesn't listen to me. I left the opportunity open for him, but now I feel I need to close it. He doesn't love me like I think he does. I think he'll always be a cheater. All I feel is hate for him, but there is still a side of me that still loves him. I'm lost about where he is with me. Were we friends, or were we more than friends? I'm starting to think that he was like everyone else I've dealt with in my life. I felt I was used by him, too, because he went out with someone else. I'm about ready to go to his grave and drive a stake in it and close the door and tell him not to come to my house anymore, and to just close the vortex to my room so he can't come to visit me. Once a cheater, always a cheater. What do you think?

A: Some people are more prone to cheat than other people, but this doesn't mean that he didn't feel love for you. In many cases, people can't help it. Sometimes when people are having problems in their relationships, they're more likely to cheat on their partners. However, this doesn't matter now, as he passed away several years ago, so the relationship is in the past. It's time to let this go, or you run the risk of bringing the problems you had with him into your future relationships.

When we pass from this life back to spirit, we see things differently. Spirit doesn't discriminate; it loves all equally. It is not possible for him to be cheating on you now, as his spirit will naturally spend time with all the people he was connected to in his life, and spirits have no bodies, so they cannot have sex. His spirit will always be around you because the two of you were connected in life. His only wish now is to see you happy and to help you if you allow him to.

I understand that you've felt hurt, but holding on to that feeling is not doing you any good. You should always forgive; this is for your benefit, and not his, as what you put out comes back to you. What you focus on is what you will create in your life, so always forgive, and don't dwell on the negative. If you spend more time looking at the positive things, you'll attract more positive things.

Q. Hi, Suzie. I'm not happy at work. I hate going, and I don't like the people I work with, but I' am scared of leaving, as I need the money. I think I may be happier doing something else, but I don't know what. Can you offer me any advice?

A. I think that no matter what you're doing, you always have choices. You can choose to be happy or not happy, to look at the positives or look at the negatives. There is good and bad to any work, or anything, for that matter. What you see is all in your attitude. I love what I do, and I make good money doing it, but there are times when I don't feel like doing it because I'm tired or sick or just wanting to be doing something else. You need to look at all of your options and at the reasons why you're not happy. You can either let other energies affect you, or you can affect them, or a combination of both can happen. Ultimately, the choice is yours.

Taking pride in your work and doing your best no matter what can be very satisfying, regardless of the job you have. Do what you love by loving what you do. If you're not happy doing what you do, then you don't need to change your job, you just need to change your attitude towards it. You'll always need to do some things whether you want to or not, and whether we prioritize them or put them off, they still need to be done. We can love doing something one day and be sick of it another. Your perception can change in the blink of an eye, but only you can change it. It is just as easy to look for the positives in any work we do as it is to look at the negatives.

The real question is, what would you prefer at this time? Would you prefer to look at the positive side of things and be happy or look at the negatives and be unhappy? Which emotions are you feeding now? If you want to enjoy what you do, then the only thing stopping you is yourself. Change the way you look at things, and the things you look at change.

If you're nice to your co-workers and treat them how you would like them, to treat you, then you may find that you get on with them better, as people like being around positive energy, and when you put out positive energy, it attracts positive energy back to you. Think about how you treat your co-workers and the energy you put out towards them. Try not to complain about them, and try to look for the positives instead of the negatives at work.

You may decide to leave this job, but before you do, think carefully about what you think you'd like to do instead, and then take steps to move your intention in that direction. You may need to study in order to have a better chance of doing what you want to do. We are always taken to where we need to be when we need to be there. If another job is meant to happen, then it will find you, and the doors will be open. Our only choice is how we travel and what we take with us. Your greater purpose is already in you, and like a flower, it will bloom when you're ready.

Q. I've been told that I'm psychic, and I was wondering if you could explain why some people are psychic and some are not, and what the purpose of being psychic is.

A. We are all psychic! These abilities are inbuilt. So many people simply don't realize this. The greater purpose of being psychic is to be more aware and more conscious of ourselves and our environment so that we can live a happier, safer, healthier existence and so we can help others to do the same. Many people do not live their greater purpose, as they are ignorant of the facts. Years of persecution changed much of society's perception and encouraged people to be ignorant; however, there has been an awakening of the mind in humans, and many people are now just starting to learn how to connect with these inbuilt abilities. Some of us are further down the path than others, and it is we who light the way for others to follow. We each have a different purpose and travel different paths, but we all meet in the same place at the end.

We are all both students and masters at the same time and are therefore equal in many ways. We can always learn and always improve, and we can all help others by teaching and demonstrating and showing them the way.

Q. What is your take on orbs? I have researched this and found a lot of evidence that explains how orbs appear in photos. Why do so many people believe that orbs in photos are spirits?

A. Many people believe in spirits, yet many people don't see spirit. When we ask for signs from spirit, we must accept that these signs may come in any form. We may see or hear something that reminds us of someone who has passed, and we may choose to believe it is coincidence, or we may choose to take it as a sign. I have met a few people who have told me that they've seen an orb, and there are countless other stories just like theirs, and then there are all of the photographs of orbs. Just to clarify, science has found many causes of orbs, including light reflecting on dust or insects or on the camera's lens. However, many people believe that orbs are actually spirits showing themselves in the form of an orb. In many photographs, faces or figures can be seen within an orb. Is this spirit, or are we just making shapes out of clouds?

I think that most people do realize that most orbs in pictures can be explained by science, but they also know that science hasn't explained everything. Therefore, they feel that it is possible that spirit can appear in orb form and it is feasible to them that some pictures of orbs in photos may actually be spirit caught in a picture. I'm open to the idea that some photos of orbs may actually be spirit, as I see and talk to spirits. Many people consider me crazy for this, but we are all free to form our own opinions. I have learnt to be open to others' ideas and to respect their right to believe what they choose to. I don't care what others think of my belief, for it is mine and not theirs. I don't try to force what I believe onto others. If someone has a belief that makes them feel happy or comforted, then I am happy for them, and whether they are right or wrong doesn't matter.

Often when I see orbs in photos near a person, I may pick up on a relative of that person. This could be that I'm sensing that spirit around that person and that it has nothing to do with there being an orb in the picture, or it could be that that spirit caused the dust or water particle to flare when the light from a flash went off, or any number of other reasons. I am not so quick to dismiss that orbs and spirits may be connected in some way, but I realize that anyone looking at orbs from a scientific view point will see only the facts that they know and will dismiss any other possible theories. Sometimes when I see an orb in a picture, it is obvious to me that it is caused by a reflection of light, but other times, I do feel spirit connected to the picture. These, of course, are only my thoughts. Please feel free to believe whatever you choose.

Q. Suzie, I would like some advice from you, if you don't mind. I'm doing my first platform readings at a spiritualist church service in July. I've never been formerly trained, and all I've done are one-to-one readings. Is there any advice you can give me?

A. I never had any training either. I like to hold people's hands, as this helps me make a good connection with them. When doing psychic stage shows, where possible, I also like to get the person I'm reading for to come up the front so I can focus on him or her properly, as sometimes multiple spirits want to connect with a person, or for different people which can be a bit confusing, and getting the person next to me helps me to connect to just them better. However, all mediums have their own styles. Just do what you find most comfortable for you. Feel the fear, but do it anyway. Trust in spirit and your ability to connect.

If you get something wrong for that person, you may be right but they're not thinking clearly and don't make the connection at the time, or the information you pick up may mean something for someone else who is there. In these cases, I just let it go and move on to the next thing I pick up.

Not everyone will connect with your energy. If you get someone you're not making a good connection with, it may be best to say so and find someone else who you make a better connection with. Always be compassionate about how you word information, speak from the heart with love, and speak with confidence. Have fun and enjoy yourself. A little humour can keep things light. I'm sure you'll do great.

Q. Hi, Suzie. Do you know a lot about ghosts and spirits? When I meditate, sometimes I feel as if something is there! Can spirits be created by visualizing them? I'm starting to read about sigils and spirits. Is this dangerous? Can casting a prayer or spell be dangerous?

A. Yes, I do know a lot about ghosts. I work as a medium, so I deal with spirits on a daily basis. When we feel like something is there, we're often correct! It is possible for you to connect with a spirit by visualizing it and having the intent to connect with that spirit. This is not normally dangerous if you know what you're doing and understand how these things work. The energy that you put out is very important. If you vibrate positive energy that is soft, gentle, loving, respectful, pure, strong, and secure, then you will attract similar energies. But if you are putting out negative energy, this will also be attracted back to you. Remember that everything is both positive and negative, and if you focus on the positive energy you're emitting and seek the positive side of what you're trying to connect with, then you can connect to the positive side of any spirit.

It also helps to understand a bit about psychic protection so that you can protect and cleanse your energy as well. There is information about this in my book.

I see spells and prayers as much like emitting a specific energy in order to obtain a specific outcome, or focusing your intention out into the universe in a clear, concise way so that the universe can help you obtain your desires and needs. If done in the right way with positive energy, you can expect positive results. A lot depends on the type of spell or prayer and the energy that you give to it. In most cases, I would say this is not dangerous, but it is always better to have some knowledge about what you're doing and what the possible consequences are. If you work with love, compassion, respect, and knowledge, then you can't go wrong.

Spirits and angels are everywhere! You only need to tune into their frequency to connect with them.

Q. Hi, Suzie. I'm also a medium, but lately, my readings have dried up, and I haven't been getting a lot of work. How do you advertise yourself to attract so many clients? Can you give me any advice or suggest any good magazines that I could advertise in to help me get more business?

A. I don't do any advertising besides placing a small ad in the psychic directory a few times over the years and once I placed an ad in *Cleo* magazine. I don't think I've gotten any readings from having these ads, and I find that when I advertise my shows in newspapers, I don't get a big response from those either. I think all of my clients come from word-of-mouth advertising, which is always the best form of advertising. One thing that has worked for me in the past were flyers, I made up a few hundred and drop some around at some local hairdressers. It is a cheap and effective way of getting word of mouth advertising started for you.

Q. Hi, Suzie. Do you ever get information for yourself, or do you only able to pick things up for others? How do you recognize the information you get, and how do you know you're not just imagining it?

A. I do pick things up for myself and for people around me all the time from spirit and my guides. My husband and children can't keep anything from me. I always know what presents I'll get. There are no secrets in my home, and I'm not often surprised. My guides are constantly telling me things that are about to happen in my life or letting me know that I'm heading in the right direction. They show me images in my mind, put thoughts into my head, give me feelings, and even talk to me as a person would. I often receive their messages as a combination of all of these things. When I'm thinking about something or talking to my husband about our plans, my guides will flicker the lights when they agree with what we're saying or what I'm thinking. Whenever a big positive change is about to happen in my life, my guides will do something to really get my attention to let me know about it. I work so much with my guides and spirits that it's easy for me to recognize the difference between their messages and my own thoughts and imagination. You just need to be open and trust in spirit and let go of your own thoughts.

Q. Hi, Suzie. What abilities do you have, and how do they work?

A. As you know, I'm a spirit medium and also psychic. As a psychic, I'm able to pick up information through my psychic senses. I see images in my mind with my third eye; these images flash through my mind. I hear voices say a single word or a name, and I hear noises, such as the engine of a plane or motorbike or the ocean or something else that means something for the person I'm doing a reading for. Sometimes I'll even smell or taste things. Often I'll feel sensations in my body that relate to something I'm picking up on. Thoughts will pop into my mind, and I may feel that I just know something. The information I pick up for people comes to me through some or all of these psychic senses, and it could relate to the past, present, or future, and I'll have a sense of which it is.

In addition to being psychic, I am also a medium, so I am able to connect with the spirits of people who have passed over. Often I'll see them standing beside the person I am reading for, and I'll hear them talk to me. but the communication more often comes through my psychic senses. I also read palms and do tarot card spreads. To do this, you simply need to learn what all of the different shapes and lines on the hand mean or what all of the different cards mean and mean when they're in a specific position in a spread. When using tools like cards or palmistry, I also pick up information from my psychic senses that adds more depth to the reading.

Q. Hi, Suzie. How can I book a reading with you? Do you have a cancellation list? Do you need a deposit?

A. I am booked out a long way in advance, so once you book in, you'll have to wait for your appointment date to come around. You can book in for a face-to-face reading, or, if you can't make it to me, you can book in for a phone or Skype reading. You can keep an eye on my website and Facebook page to see when I have live shows coming up. I do have a cancellation waiting list, but it is pages of names, and I don't get many cancellations, which means that getting a booking this way is a bit like winning the lottery. I don't require a deposit; just pay on the day. I call a few days before the appointment to confirm details with you. If you can't make your appointment, I can always try to swap you with someone else so you don't need to wait.

Thank you

We are all connected, yet we are individuals. There is still much we all can experience to prosper, grow, and learn from our journeys in this life and the next.

Ghost Whisperer Suzie: Heaven on Earth takes you on a journey through Suzie Price's life experiences, thoughts, and beliefs about psychic development and many other spiritual topics so that you can better understand your path in life.

Join Suzie as she shares her highs and lows through her experiences with depression, anxiety, and nervous breakdowns to living a happy and successful life in her own little piece of Heaven on Earth!

Suzie Price
Ghost Whisperer Suzie,
International Psychic Medium
Spiritual Teacher
Singer-songwriter
Author
www.ghostwhisperersuzie.com.au
www.facebook.com/ghostwhisperersuzie
www.youtube.com/user/ghostwhisperersuzie